We live in an increasingly low-trust world. For too many, morale is suffering, engagement is dismal, and inspiration is lacking. *Appreciate* shows leaders how to counteract this by intentionally building powerful, authentic, high-trust relationships with their teams.

Stephen M.R. Covey
New York Times best-selling Author of
The Speed of Trust and coauthor of *Smart Trust*

Appreciate provides a practical guide to becoming a great leader and a clear path to enabling a vibrant company culture. Companies that embrace these core principles will naturally increase their employee engagement, productivity and innovation, a goal that all companies aspire to. This is a must read for any leader looking to increase their impact.

Kumar Kymal
Senior Vice President, HR-Corporate Functions & Total Rewards
Thomson Reuters

In a business world awash with leadership models, competencies, tools and advice, *Appreciate* stands out. It humanizes leadership theory by touching the core of what matters most to people in their personal and working lives—the need for validation of their self-worth, to be valued. The positive connection between recognition, engagement, and great work performance is beyond question. *Appreciate* is an invaluable resource for leaders aiming to inspire people to produce great work.

Deirdre Lander
Director Data, Surveys and Technology
Willis Towers Watson Hong Kong

Having had the opportunity to read *Appreciate: Celebrating People, Inspiring Greatness*, I was impressed by the quality of the management advice. This is well written, easy to grasp, and a great reminder, for any manager at any level, of our most important asset—our people. I will keep it close by.

Daniel Lamarre
President & CEO
Cirque du Soleil

The most important role a leader plays is his or her ability to inspire and energize the team. In today's results-oriented business climate, appreciation and support are one of the most powerful tools we have to keep people charging ahead to learn, grow, and meet business demands.

Josh Bersin
Principal and Founder
Bersin by Deloitte

Great book! Simple philosophy. Brilliant practice. We often get stuck focusing on the policies, procedures, and business systems of work, but forget the fact that we're all just people trying to do great work. *Appreciate* clearly shows why not forgetting this is the most vital bit!

Prabir Jha
President & Global Chief People Officer
Cipla

As an organization, we know from first-hand experience that recognition is a key driver of engagement. It inspires our employees to give their best at work every day, and this book provides a clear and concise plan that any company can use to build a fantastic culture of appreciation.

Carolyn Clark
Senior Vice President, Talent & Culture, North & Central America
Accor Hotels

Appreciate is nourishment for the workplace soul. It will transform the way you perceive your role as a leader, and the growth of the people around you.

James D. White
Former Chairman, President & CEO
Jamba Juice

As a student of servant leadership, *Appreciate* is a must read for all that truly want to lead and build great teams. Catching people doing things right is a powerful leadership tool. *Appreciate* is a great tool to have ordinary people perform at extraordinary levels.

Bill Fields
Shop Keeper
Chairman at Fields Texas Limited Inc.
and Former CEO of Walmart Stores Division

As a Human Resources executive, I read a lot of books on leadership. I have to say that *Appreciate* is my new favorite! I love the concept of leadership's role in creating appreciation "moments" for others, that in turn inspire individuals to achieve results. Appreciation is a simple, but not always easy concept. *Appreciate* provides leaders an effective play book to make this part of how they show up with their teams every day, and how they can unleash their teams' abilities to truly make a difference within their organizations.

Laurie Miller
Executive Vice President Human Resources
Alliance HealthCare Services

One of the most powerful services we can offer another human being is the acknowledgment, recognition, and sincere appreciation for great work. This book reveals the profound impact of appreciation in all societies, and a clear and concise roadmap of how you can apply it to your leadership and your culture.

Ron Kaufman
New York Times best-selling Author of
Uplifting Service

Having the best talent is not enough! *Appreciate* is a critical book to help unlock the embedded energy within all levels of talent. This is an excellent guide to understand why and how appreciation kindles the passion within all of us.

Victor Buzachero
Senior Vice President
Scripps Health

Lots of companies talk about investing in their people. Sure, money talks, but so do actions. *Appreciate* shows how companies can act and organize to value employee contributions. In fact, my research shows that appreciation-rich companies outperform companies that take employees for granted. Every leader needs to read this book!

L.J. Rittenhouse
CEO Rittenhouse Rankings, Inc.
and *New York Times* and Wall Street Journal best-selling Author of
Investing Between the Lines

We live in a fast-paced world where everyone is focused on moving forward. And, we often forget, or don't know how to effectively recognize, all the people in our lives that make us better. *Appreciate* shows us how; everyday and everywhere!

Robin Verboom
Compensation & Benefits and Global Mobility
Fiat Chrysler Automobiles, Italy

Read *Appreciate* to learn how to influence and inspire your organization to create a culture of great work. Regardless of your leadership level, this book is a powerful tool that will help you achieve results.

Healy MacPhail
Vice President Human Resources
Alliance HealthCare Services

No one ever went broke giving appreciation. In a concise and definitive manner, *Appreciate* shows the power and impact this simple act can give to creating world-class influencers who can lead any industry.

Jay Samit
New York Times best-selling Author of
Disrupt You!

We live in a complex world and our businesses are rapidly evolving but there is great simplicity that never changes and that is engaging and enlivening human spirit. Leaders aspiring to be memorable and impactful will pick up *Appreciate* and apply the lessons, information and research. I recommend this resource to anyone trying to make a difference in their relationships and workplace!

Dana Ullom-Vucelich
Chief Human Resources & Ethics Officer
Ohio Living

As leaders continue to navigate the different generations in the workplace engaging all employees is a critical component to success. *Appreciate* is a great resource with practical tips on how to appreciate, inspire, and ensure great work. I highly recommend it.

Cara Williams
Human Resource Executive
Scripps Health

If you want to lead, you need to read *Appreciate*. This is a simple roadmap to engaging, inspiring, and influencing great work from your people.

Marshall Goldsmith
Ranked #1 Leadership Coach and
Author of *Triggers*

Appreciate highlights the critical role appreciation plays in influencing great work and provides the practical framework for this essential foundation of an inspiring company culture. I recommend this book to anyone who aspires to be a leader.

Dan McNamee
President
Floyd's 99 Barbershops

Better than a business strategy, *Appreciate* not only gives us a roadmap to improve our communication and relationships at work, but it also helps us to focus on, and align, values. This book could transform an entire culture.

Ann Rhoades
CEO of People Ink
Co-Founder Jet Blue and
Author of *Built on Values*

A necessary and welcome message! While many of us focus on what we can become in life, *Appreciate* shows us how to elevate the world around us. This is a must read for every leader.

Grady Lee
CEO
Give2Get

This book supports the fundamental truth about work: employee satisfaction is directly linked to customer satisfaction and profitability. Companies that understand this appreciate their employees in many different ways; those that don't will not be able to compete or survive. This is a must read for business leaders at all levels.

Arte Nathan
President, Strategic Development Worldwide
former CHRO of Wynn Resorts

This book made me realize the impact appreciation has had in my life, and the significant role I can play in the lives of others. Words have immense power. *Appreciate* helps us become aware of using our words in the most impactful ways.

Arun Rao
Head of Human Resources, India
DXC Technology

APPRECIATE

APPRECIATE

CELEBRATING PEOPLE
INSPIRING GREATNESS

DAVID STURT TODD NORDSTROM
KEVIN AMES GARY BECKSTRAND

O.C. Tanner Institute Publishing
1930 South State Street
Salt Lake City, Utah 84115

For information about special discounts for bulk purchases, please contact inquiries@octanner.com.

The O.C. Tanner Institute can bring authors to your live event. For more information or to book an event, contact speaking@octanner.com.

First O.C. Tanner Institute Publishing hardcover edition 2017

Printed in the United States of America

Library of Congress Control Number: 2017934223

ISBN-13: 978-0-9969808-0-7
ISBN-10: 0-9969808-0-6

eISBN-13: 978-0-9969808-1-4
eISBN-10: 0-9969808-1-4

Audiobook-13: 978-0-9969808-2-1
Audiobook-10: 0-9969808-2-2

There is nothing louder than the silence where thanks should be.

CONTENTS

CONTENTS

THE POWER OF A WORD

The sound of corduroy trousers brushed rhythmically from the back of the class as the professor approached Todd's desk. The soles of his leather shoes softly tapped the tiles. They were innocent sounds, but Todd was terrified.

The professor stopped, loudly sighing as he placed Todd's paper face down on the front corner of his desk. Was he frustrated with Todd's work? Did the paper not meet the professor's expectations? Up until now, Todd had been getting straight A's in the class.

"Please see me after class," said the professor, as he tapped his knuckles on Todd's paper.

This was a moment of truth. It was one of those instances that reveal if we are, in fact, the people we hope we are. In baseball, a moment of truth requires us to step up to the plate. And, within a matter of a few pitches, we come to know if we're in the game, or out. As a writer, as well as with most other professions, the lines are not always so clear. There isn't always an umpire telling you if you've struck out. There isn't usually a loud crack of the bat that sends your work soaring into bright lights. In fact, writers—like most other professions—are measured on a different set of criteria. The number of words doesn't matter. The speed at which they write doesn't matter. What is important is the impact the words have on the reader.

What matters is the difference the words make in people's lives. And, unlike a baseball player, a writer doesn't typically get to hear the roaring cheers from the fans.

Consider the books you love. Most likely, you will never meet their authors. You will not have the opportunity to congratulate them for writing such vivid prose the way Ernest Hemingway could almost make a reader taste the smoke of a cigar and smell the stench of a dead fish.

Todd wanted to be such a writer—to inspire readers to feel a character's intense love, or tremble with fear, or see the world with new eyes. He wanted to be great with words—not just with the technical aspects of grammar, punctuation, and style, but with creating impact, making a difference in his readers' lives.

"I want to thank every one of you for being in my class," said the professor, after he had laid each student's paper on their desk. "Best of luck to all of you in all your future endeavors."

Most of the students in class lunged toward the door. To them, the class was simply another hurdle on their way to a degree. For Todd, the stakes were much higher. So, as all the other students crowded the exit, Todd sat motionless in his seat, still terrified to turn over his paper and read the professor's remarks.

"You're not in a rush?" the professor asked, packing his teaching materials into a weathered leather satchel. Then he noticed Todd had not turned his paper over. "You haven't looked at your grade yet?" he asked.

Todd looked up. "You read *The Great Gatsby*," the professor said. "You really read it. You read it the way it should be read." He smiled. Then he paused, biting his lower lip as if he was searching for words.

"Todd, I've been teaching this class for a very long time," he said. "I wish I could write the way you write." The professor then nodded at the paper, suggesting that Todd should turn it over. Next to a large red "A" at the top, one word was written: "Beautiful."

Todd admits that he got a little choked-up when he saw that word. It was almost as if the professor understood him on a deeper level— as if he was aware of who Todd wanted to be, what he wanted to be appreciated for, and how hard he had worked to find just the right insights and combination of words. It was as if the professor knew Todd had chosen him as the litmus test to decide whether or not Todd could write a good paper or an excellent paper. "The thing I don't think he realized was that I would be thinking about his comments more than twenty years later," said Todd. "That day in class, that one written word became a symbol for my work." Even today, before starting a new piece of writing, Todd finds himself thinking, "Strive for beautiful."

We all have these experiences—these moments in life that affect us in a profoundly meaningful way. Maybe for you it happened in elementary school when a teacher commented on your artwork or mathematical abilities. Or maybe praise came from a middle-school music instructor who applauded your creative confidence, or from a respected teammate who gave you an approving nod on the sports field. Alternatively, maybe you recall a manager early in your career recognizing a particular thing you did well, possibly even pointing out a talent you had wondered about but hadn't fully discovered yet.

After interviewing hundreds of people in all kinds of professions, we have yet to come across someone who doesn't have one of these stories. These are the moments and experiences that have shaped you; they have inspired and encouraged you to become who you are today.

These experiences, like Todd's, are rarely the stories that get repeated in company meetings or conference rooms, or get retold because of their grandiose outcomes. These stories rarely show how one person revolutionized the world, or saved a life, or faced insurmountable challenges, or even survived horrible circumstances to find success. However, these are the stories that are the building blocks and inflection points of the great things that follow. They are found deep within each of us, quietly guiding and influencing what we do and what we believe we are capable of accomplishing. These are the stories that, day in and day out, inspire and fuel your personal greatness.

For Todd, that single word from his professor, "Beautiful," became a catalyst for his career. Similar expressions or comments in your life have had, and will have, a similar effect. When you really understand the impact an appreciative comment has had on your life and career, then are you able to see the extraordinary influence you can have on others.

We, along with a talented team of researchers, conduct some of the world's largest workplace studies. We interview people across the globe—from leaders of many of the world's most respected companies to frontline employees from every walk of life. We have spent years researching the personal experiences and moments at work that change people and affect the work they do.

As you explore the insights in this book, we hope you'll come to better understand a profoundly powerful motivating force in our lives: people's desire to make a difference through their work—a difference that is valued and appreciated.

This book will provide you with insights, stories, and concrete steps on how you can become a great leader and inspire the "beautiful" in those you lead.

CHAPTER 1

IT'S UNIVERSAL

To appreciate, quite simply, means to apply wisdom, sound judgment, and keen insight in recognizing the value of someone or something.[1] Think about it. The feeling of appreciation comes from experiencing something great, something that inspires you, something that moves you, and something that benefits you or others. And the deeper the sense of appreciation you feel, the greater the effect someone's action has had upon you. That's a powerful thing.

Imagine, for a second, that you were in the audience listening to Beethoven's Ninth Symphony on its opening night, May 7, 1824.[2] After the performance, the entire crowd leapt to their feet—some were even weeping. Surely, the entire audience was enraptured by the extraordinary work of the maestro. It's said that the audience's response at this performance was spontaneous, elicited by the indescribable music. Beethoven's work doesn't stand alone for being appreciated. The same phenomenon has, to varying degrees, and by various artists, been repeated over and over again across genres, venues, and performances around the world. Coldplay's Chris Martin, some may suggest, cannot be categorized with the likes of Beethoven. However, when an eight-year-old boy's father recently filmed his autistic son's emotional reaction during a Coldplay concert in Mexico City, the video instantly went viral, exposing the profound impact appreciation has on the human spirit. And, ironically, the feeling of appreciation was shared by all—the boy appreciating the music and the band appreciating the boy's reaction. Coldplay was actually so touched by the video that they tweeted, "This kind of thing makes it all worthwhile. Hola Luis y tu hijo hermoso! Love cgwj&p."[3]

We, as human beings, simply can't help it. When we are in the presence of great work, we cannot help but feel a profound sense of appreciation for it. It somehow touches a place in the human spirit that elevates us. It raises our heartbeat. It inspires us to become better. And leaves us tongue-tied, trying to decipher a definition for our sense of awe.

When we watched the opening scene of the original *Star Wars* movie for the first time, we sat spellbound, riveted, with a sense of thrill and wonder—and we weren't alone. George Lucas and his team had introduced the world to new levels of stunning imagery, life-like realism, and imaginative characters that delighted hundreds of millions of people around the globe. Ultimately, the appreciation of the first movie provoked the demand for more movies, resulting in one of the most prolific film franchises ever made.

Or consider how, after trying for 108 years, the Chicago Cubs won the 2016 World Series and the entire country cheered.[4] Not because they were all Cubs fans, but because we love witnessing greatness. We love to be in the presence of ordinary people doing extraordinary things or overcoming extraordinary obstacles. We relish the achievement—often with people we don't know, because, well, somehow we can all relate to the work, the sacrifice, the setbacks, and the utter desire to accomplish something magnificent.

This desire, and the appreciation of great accomplishment, isn't new. It dates to the earliest recordings in human history—in every endeavor, and every culture.

DEEP IN EVERYBODY'S SOCIETAL ROOTS

The admiration and respect for accomplishment is embedded deep in the core of every society known to mankind. In fact, the appreciation of great work has underscored and punctuated every dimension of human existence since the beginning of time.

In the oldest archaeological sites, ancient paintings on cave walls describe and illustrate the actions of hunters and gatherers of their day. In one of the largest caves in Bulgaria, the Magura Cave drawings depict humans hunting and dancing over their prey—a symbol of accomplishment.[5] We see it in ancient Rome and Athens on stone monuments that celebrate victories in battle, acts of valor, and other accomplishments worthy of their people's respect and admiration.

When communities dedicate common areas for public grounds, they usually include some expression of appreciation for the work of those who made those areas possible. In cities throughout Europe, for example, squares and public spaces prominently feature statues and monuments to honor heroic men and women whose deeds were deserving of public appreciation. Consider the public grounds in your city or town. They are named after people who built or saved villages, leaders that united or persevered, and activists who often risked their own safety or reputation for the greater good.

In South America, atop Mount Corcovado in the glistening harbor of Rio De Janeiro, stands a massive statue of Jesus Christ called the *Cristo Redentor,* Christ the Redeemer. Why did the people of Rio deem it worthy of such an enormous tribute? It was because of the work and words of one whose influence changed the course of human history. It serves as a reminder of not only what people in that area believe in, but what they value—great works that inspire us all.

On yet another continent, in Australia's Sydney harbor, proudly stands the Sydney Opera House, an iconic landmark acclaimed for being the architectural icon of the 20th century. The structure, which took sixteen years to build, created architectural challenges that had never been witnessed before. In fact, the technical challenge of creating the iconic roof sails took a full four years to solve. Why go through so much effort?[6]

In North America, on Ellis Island in New York, stands the most recognized icon of American freedom, the Statue of Liberty. What you may not know, however, is that Lady Liberty also represents an act of appreciation. Of course, many people know the statue was a gift from France, but most don't know *why* the gift was given.

Edouard de Laboulaye, born in Paris in 1811 to a wealthy family, studied law and became passionate about understanding U.S. government, which was still relatively new at the time. Through his career and the publication of many papers and books, the shy Frenchman gained a deep appreciation for the ideals of U.S. government: freedom, liberty, and democracy.

On numerous occasions, Laboulaye tried to bring this passion to the French government. He ran for political office several times and lost. Nevertheless, his appreciation for the ideology of freedom ended up having a greater influence on the world than he ever imagined. Believing the world would understand the power of democracy if they could see a symbol of it, in 1865 Laboulaye pitched the idea for the Statue of Liberty to the French government. She would be a gift to their ally, the United States of America, as a symbol of their deep mutual appreciation for democracy.[7]

All over the world we can see similar examples of significant expressions of appreciation. In Nobel Square in Cape Town, South Africa, stands a statue of Nelson Mandela. The statue memorializes the extraordinary influence of a man's life work, a work that transformed an entire nation by bringing about a peaceful transition to a democratic government in South Africa. Ironically, that statue stands directly across the bay from Robben Island and the prison where Mandela was incarcerated for twenty-seven years during his relentless pursuit of his people's freedom. Standing with Mandela's statue are three other recipients of the Nobel Prize: F.W. de Klerk, who partnered with Mandela to end apartheid and allow for the transition to democracy, Albert Luthuli, and Archbishop Emeritus Desmond Tutu. "These men all played their part in helping South Africa to democracy after decades of apartheid."[8]

It's not only through things—statues, monuments, and prizes—that we express our appreciation. We love to celebrate great accomplishments in many other ways, too. The tradition of ticker-tape parades in New York City has been going on since the very first impromptu paper-dropping celebration happened in 1886 to honor the dedication of the Statue of Liberty. Since then, athletes, astronauts, civic leaders, and other notable figures have received tons of confetti dropped on their parades.[9]

The Nobel Prize, instituted in 1895, is one of the world's most prestigious examples of appreciating great work. It honors those who have influenced others on a global level in the fields of chemistry, literature, peace, physics, physiology, and medicine. Its honorees include Albert Einstein, Ernest Hemingway, Martin Luther King Jr., Gertrude B. Elion, Marie Curie, and many more.

But the Nobel Prize is just one of many awards of appreciation. We find it fascinating that our societies have instituted contests and awards that celebrate every aspect of great accomplishment. There are the Olympics for sport, Oscars for film, Emmys for television, Grammys for music, Pulitzers for writing, and the list goes on and on. In the business world, Fortune honors the top 100 most admired companies as best places to work. In the culinary world, one of our favorite awards is the Meilleur Ouvrier de France, otherwise known as the MOF Award. Offered every four years, a jury judges each chef's technical skill, innovation, and respect for tradition to ensure every aspect repeatedly meets a certain level of refinement, excellence, effectiveness, and quickness. The reason we love the award so much is that sometimes there isn't a winner. In fact, in 2015, no MOF chocolatier was awarded because no one met the minimum score required.[10]

In education, honorary degrees are given to people whose contributions to a specific field or to society in general are noteworthy. In some countries, people who achieve distinguished achievements are knighted. Knighthood is bestowed only upon those whose actions were remarkable, brave, or committed to serving the country and its people.[11]

Closer to everyday life, school hallways are adorned with plaques on walls and portraits of past principals or students who achieved great things. There are trophies in cabinets that tell stories of victories, honors, and accomplishments since the school first opened. They serve as reminders of moments of greatness and as inspiration to new generations of students and teachers.

Even our homes are graced with symbols of appreciation—art on the walls, children's art on the fridge, framed photos of those whose influence and friendship you appreciate. On children's dressers we find memorabilia that tell stories of that which they value and appreciate. And take a look at nearly anyone's Facebook, LinkedIn, or Instagram pages. You'll quickly discover photos of our achievements, those of friends and family, and even our pets. "Look, my dog Frisbee learned to shake hands today."

WE ARE ALL FANS OF GREAT WORK

Why do we find ourselves replaying video highlights of Lionel Messi's greatest goals? Or watching YouTube videos of surfers catching gnarly waves, tightrope walks across canyons, or musicians playing instruments in unexpected and extraordinary ways? Why do we stay up late into the night to watch cyclists in the Tour de France cross the finish line? Could it be that we crave sharing the moment of victory so we can vicariously feel what the victor feels? To experience the emotional surge of accomplishment? When the contest is over we want to relive each of the great moments. We cringe when things go badly, and our hearts sing when we watch the impossible landing or the flawless performance on the mat. We watch in slow motion the final stroke and touch of the wall in the swimming pool, appreciating every angle, every split second of the experience. Just as important, we celebrate the winner's victory. And we also shed tears when someone experiences a heartbreaking loss, because in some deeply human way we can relate to their pain. These priceless images—the effort, the sweat, the aspiration, and the achievement—transform us all. They show us what is possible. They remind us of the greatness of the human spirit—that the work and sacrifice was worth it. And they refuel our lives and inspire us to dream.

Watching people do great things influences the wiring in our own brains. We came across some fascinating research from the University of Southern California that shows what happens to our own brains when we feel appreciation or gratitude.[12] In the study, participants were asked to watch video vignettes of Holocaust survivors who shared moments of gratitude surrounding the event. Some spoke of strangers who hid or protected them during Nazi manhunts. Others commented on smaller things they appreciated, like receiving a loaf of bread or the mere pleasure of sleeping on a bed for a night.

Twenty-three participants watched forty-eight vignettes while they were connected to a brain scanner. The results were fascinating. "There seems to be a thread that runs through subtle acts of gratitude, such as holding a door for someone, all the way up to the big powerful stuff like when someone gives you a kidney," said Glenn Fox, a postdoctoral researcher at USC and lead author of the study. "I designed this experiment to see what aspects of brain function are common to both these small feelings of appreciation and large feelings of gratitude."

Researchers found that participants experienced enhanced brain activity in two primary regions: the anterior cingulate cortex and the medial prefrontal cortex. These areas of the brain are associated with emotional processing, interpersonal bonding, and rewarding so-cial interactions. But here is where the study gets really interesting. "A lot of people conflate gratitude with the simple emotion of receiving a nice thing. What we found was something a little more interesting," said Fox. "The pattern of [brain] activity we see shows that gratitude is a complex social emotion that is really built around how others seek to benefit us."

Our research confirms this. Appreciation and gratitude is far more complex than someone receiving a nice thing—it's a connection between two or more people that benefits everyone, including the person sharing their appreciation or gratitude. The study proves the impactful benefit of giving recognition, where participants who give recognition experienced a 170% increase in engagement, a 294% increase in innovation, and a 221% increase in results.[13]

In other words, appreciation isn't just about reward. In fact, it doesn't just show up in the brain's reward center. Instead, it involves morality, connecting with others, and even taking their perspective. It teaches us what it's like to be them.

IF APPRECIATION IS A TEACHER, THEN WHY DON'T WE LEARN?

As Todd's experience in the introduction shows, when someone verbalizes their appreciation of great work they shine a light not just on the work itself, but on a person's strengths, abilities, and even opportunities. Verbalizing the appreciation teaches people about their possibility for the future. If you think back to when, and how, you found out you were really good at something, the chances are high that someone pointed it out to you. They verbalized it somehow. Maybe it came through an approving nod of a fellow classmate on the school playground when you scored a goal. Maybe it came from a teacher, a relative, a friend, or a manager who told you that you showed extra potential in a certain area. Or maybe it came via winning an award, earning respect, or receiving recognition that made you realize you had a special talent. No matter when or how it happened, that instance of appreciation sent a powerful message to you about who you are, what you can do, and who you could become.

This is where the problem lies. For some reason, it's easy to look back into our own lives and replay the moments where we felt the transformative power of appreciation. It's easy to look back and see the impact it has made on our life, our work, and our career. It's easy to verbalize how much someone's words of appreciation meant to us. But, as you'll soon discover, studies show it's difficult for us to verbalize our appreciation for the people we work with, and even for those who work for us.

If we love to celebrate greatness, why aren't more celebrations happening at work? Why aren't we cheering more for the differences people make in our lives day in and day out—the guy who saved you an extra day because he went the extra mile, or the woman who made you appear brilliant because she figured out how to solve a challenging problem? Why is the workplace different? Why are employees expected to perform monumental tasks without praise? Is it because they get paid? Do we view work differently than the rest of our lives? Do we see work as simply transactional?

For some reason, the workplace hasn't followed suit with our global culture of celebrating greatness. The human desire to celebrate at work has been seemingly quashed by the expectation of progress. Workplace culture has somehow dictated that a stellar performance at work is rewarded only by a paycheck.

It's no wonder the world watches the Olympic Games with an emotional eye—that we all feel emotionally connected to athletes in random sports most of us would never consider as entertainment and that we can relate to the heartache of losing and the aspiration of winning in such an intensely human way. It's because, in a way, we are those people. The difference is many of us do not get the chance to celebrate our achievements. We don't get to cheer for our coworkers. We go to work each day seeing the effort, witnessing the struggle, experiencing the results, and watching our coworkers and employees develop into experts in their fields, and yet we rarely say a word to show our appreciation.

Appreciation lives deep within us all. It's been a foundational aspect of all recorded cultures. And although applause is almost everywhere we look and in almost every single endeavor possible, it's not everywhere it needs to be. It's all of our jobs to change that. We can influence greatness by bringing appreciation to work.

QUICK TAKE

Appreciation Is Universal

Look back through history. Appreciation is a foundational aspect of all cultures, civilizations, career fields, sports, education, and militaries throughout history. People who achieve great things are celebrated.

People Are Fans of Great Work

Something magical happens when people view others achieving great results. When we see great work, we are inspired to be part of it, relate to it, and celebrate it. In fact, studies show that the feeling of appreciation changes brain chemistry.

Appreciation Is a Teacher, But We're Not Often the Best Students

Throughout our lives we experience moments of appreciation—where someone's verbal cues have shown you the possibility of what you can do, achieve, and become. These moments boost us to new levels. They inspire us to do great work. And this great work often results in leadership roles. Sadly, many of us never learn how to show our appreciation for others and don't realize that it's our responsibility as a leader to verbalize that appreciation.

CHAPTER 2

THE ONE THING

We have yet to meet a leader who believes he or she is great at leading people. Most leaders are trying to figure out how to lead on the job. One of the most important questions being asked among new and seasoned leaders alike is "What one thing could I do as a leader to help my team accomplish our goals?" There are so many leadership skills, techniques, theories, philosophies, and practices that compete for our attention and inclusion. However, we have all come to realize that there will never be enough time in any of our lifetimes to adopt even a fraction of these skills into our leadership practices. We have also all had enough experience with the 80/20 rule to know that we have to choose our work wisely. We have to prioritize and focus our energies on the handful of highest-gain, highest-impact things we can do to achieve the results we are responsible for delivering. The key is understanding what is most important.

Often, leaders are so focused on themselves as leaders that they fail to find out what those they lead want most from them. Research becomes an incredibly insightful tool to help find answers to these questions.

In late 2015, the O.C. Tanner Institute conducted a survey of over 1,000 employees across the United States to get their perspectives on what they wanted most from their leaders.[1] Here is the specific question we asked: "What is the most important thing your manager or company does (or could do) to cause you to produce great work?"

The question was open-ended with no predefined selections to choose from, and each respondent had to write in the most important thing to them. We then read each of the responses and grouped them into common themes. The results were fascinating.

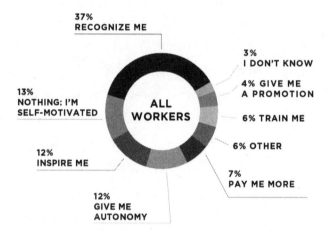

It was no surprise to see increased pay and promotions on the list. However, each of them represents surprisingly small percentage of the whole. Autonomy was also not surprising to see on the list, as people need some room to innovate and find better ways of doing things. Autonomy also communicates a certain level of trust. Another interesting finding was the importance of "inspire me" on the list. Employees are mostly absorbed by the urgencies and pressures of their day-to-day work. These respondents probably understand that inspiration is an important catalyst for their own creativity and innovation.

The most significant statistic from this research was that 37% of respondents identified recognition as the most important thing their leader or company could do to cause them to produce great work. That percentage was nearly three times larger than that of any other response in the survey.

Just as interesting, this research also found that the desire to be recognized is even stronger among younger employees. A full 41% of those aged 25–35 identified recognition as the most important action their leader could take to help them produce great work.

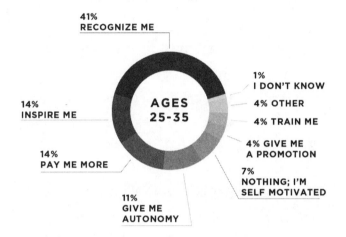

41%
RECOGNIZE ME

AGES
25-35

14%
INSPIRE ME

14%
PAY ME MORE

11%
GIVE ME
AUTONOMY

1%
I DON'T KNOW

4% OTHER

4% TRAIN ME

4% GIVE ME
A PROMOTION

7%
NOTHING; I'M
SELF MOTIVATED

So what is it about recognition and appreciation that is such an important influencer of great work? Why does it stand out above all other things leaders could do to help their team members do great work?

The answers are found in the things recognition influences. One of those is employee engagement.

The O.C. Tanner Institute, in conjunction with Towers Watson, conducted a survey of employees in thirteen countries to assess the role of appreciation in increasing employee engagement.[2] The findings proved that, wherever you are in the world, appreciation is an essential factor in employees' sense of opportunity and wellbeing, trust, and pride in the organization—all critical factors that affect employee engagement. Another key finding from this global study revealed appreciation's power to accelerate engagement—both on an individual and cultural basis. From country to country, the study showed that engagement scores were as much as two to three times higher when a leader offered specific, timely recognition that was tied to the company's core values. Moreover, it impacted all who witnessed it.

Similar results were confirmed by another global study that showed recognition for great work significantly impacts employee engagement at a rate of more than two to one.[3] Below are the comparison scores of the impact of appreciation on employee engagement in major regions of the world.

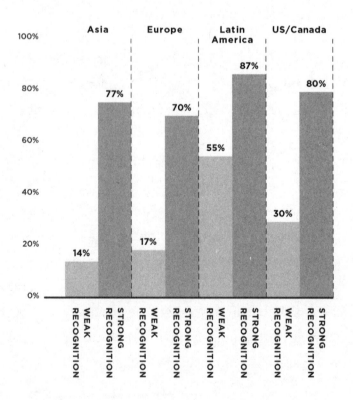

Percentage of Employees Who Are Highly Engaged

Interestingly, the same 2013 global study also showed the direct impact appreciation has on innovation and improvement.

Percentage of Employees Who Are Proactively Innovating

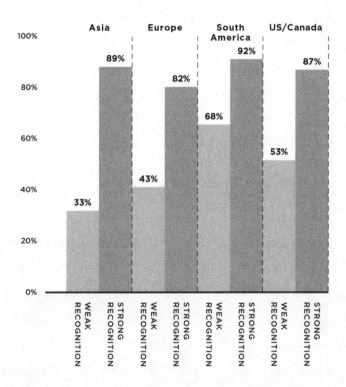

The influence of appreciating great work extends out beyond employee performance, too. In the healthcare industry, for example, effectively recognizing healthcare workers for great work has resulted in increased patient-satisfaction scores and better clinical outcomes. At Ohio Living, a regional assisted living organization with 3,000 employees, the results speak for themselves.

"We have been able to go beyond connecting great recognition practices to the typical metrics—turnover, satisfaction, engagement," says Dana Ullom-Vucelich, Chief Human Resource & Ethics Officer at Ohio Living. "Not that those things are unimportant—they are very important. However, what caught our attention is that when locations have high recognition scores, their patients also have fewer incidences of infections, pressure sores, improved health department scores, and there is greater continuity of care."[4]

Dana, like many of you, is a leader who wanted to see improvement. She experimented with her teams and groups to see what kind of impact appreciation could have, collected data that measured the benefit, and eventually rolled out changes throughout her entire organization.

Leaders in other industries are seeing similar results. Consider Dow Chemical, recognized globally as a company that intersects science and technology markets. Of course, we could talk about Dow with regard to product innovation. We could talk about the company's dedication to sustainability. And we could talk about the long list of awards for creating solutions throughout the world where they are needed the most. But the thing you might not expect to hear about Dow Chemical is how they've focused on creating a culture of recognition and appreciation.

Headquartered in Midland, Michigan, Dow Chemical has always focused on recognizing people and their talent. But as the company continued to grow throughout the world, so did the need to maintain the culture of appreciation. "Every single person has an individual motivator," said Curtis Kesler, the Recognition and Appreciation Program Manager at Dow Chemical. "There was a need to move forward with a global strategy, but with local implementation taking more of the local culture into consideration."

To accomplish this goal, Dow created strategies that would thrive in local cultures around the globe but still be part of one cohesive Dow culture. When they adjusted the way they communicate and recognize their people, the number of employees engaged in their formal recognition program, Accelerate Great, increased from just 11% in 2014 to a whopping 84% in 2015.

"When employees feel validated and feel a part of the bigger picture, and a part of the strategy, we all work harder," added Kesler. "We do more. We put more effort into everything we do and we do better work."[5]

Kesler is right. When moments of recognition and appreciation are personal and memorable they change the way people work. We have heard examples from all over the world. Each moment is meaningful in its own way, as illustrated by the following example.

Traffic was crazy. A young boy was strapped safely into his car seat, and Patricia, a young mother, was running late for an appointment. Many of us have been in this situation—little mouths are chattering in the background, stress is high, and the other cars on the freeway are uncomfortably close at high speeds.

Trying to calm her son, and maintain her nerves, Patricia was distracted. She was thinking about the consequences of missing her appointment, about how her son insisted on removing his shoes in the back seat, and about how it would add minutes to her already late timeline. She was thinking about the bright orange sports car weaving in and out of lanes ahead of her because the driver seemed frustrated by every other car on the road. The one thing Patricia was not thinking about, as her mind raced with the traffic, was her exit which was in the next lane over, blocked by a large semi-truck.

Hit the gas. Pull in front of the truck.

Patricia accelerated. Her son was chattering in the back seat. Her eyes were on the clock. And suddenly the traffic in the exit lane in front of her was at a dead stop.

Imagine for a second the thoughts running through Patricia's mind with her son in the back seat and the giant grill of the semi-truck bearing down on her. Imagine the panic. Imagine the fear.

Patricia was lucky that day. There was no accident. She was able to come to a safe, although tense, stop and so was the truck driver behind her.

Feeling a sense of relief as she sat in gridlock traffic, Patricia looked in the rear-view mirror to see the driver of the truck. He did not seem panicked at all. The driver did not seem shocked or stunned or even affected by the near collision. In fact, he appeared calm and collected.

Patricia also noticed the logo on the truck that day—it was the same company her mother worked for in the company's training department. Patricia called her mom and told her about the incident. She explained how, despite her dangerous move, the driver had been attentive and proactively prepared to respond flawlessly. Patricia described how he had anticipated the situation and how his job—as a professional driver—is most likely the reason Patricia and her son are alive today. In fact, Patricia was so relieved the driver had done his job so well she quickly wrote down his license number and wrote a letter to him to express her appreciation.

Of course, this was not an incident that Patricia's mother felt she could let go unappreciated either. So she watched the driver's schedule to find out the next time he would be in the office. She approached him the next time he was there and told him how grateful she was that he was behind the wheel that day. She explained how any other untrained or distracted driver might have killed her daughter and grandchild—and it was all because he did his job well.

Think about it. Most truck drivers are not the recipients of any appreciation at work as they spend many hours alone on the road. Their skills and attention to detail may not often receive praise as those of us on the road around them often assume that they're simply sharing the road the same way we share the road. And we might continue to make the assumption that we're all the same until we see that monster grill and bumper approaching the back of our car at high speed.

As Patricia's mother relayed this story to us, she said the burly truck driver became emotional over her gratitude and words of appreciation. In fact, overwhelmed by Patricia's mother's words, the driver said it was the first time anyone in the company had told him he had done something right.

We have been astounded by the lasting effect of moments of appreciation like these. If the truck driver is like most people we have interviewed, he will hang on to Patricia's letter for years to come. And, based on our research, we can confidently predict this driver will become even better and more attentive on the road merely because someone appreciated what he did that day.

Think back on your own moments of appreciation in school, at work, in your family, or in the community. What words has someone shared with you that made you feel appreciated? You remember them. You can recall the words, how they were said and how they made you feel. In these moments, a powerful energy connects you to the person, team, or company and your work. These moments help you overcome your doubts, fears, and anxieties about whether or not you're good at what you do. They are the moments that quash your worries and make you realize you want to keep improving for the future. It may just be a few simple but directed words, but these are the moments you realize your work, talents, and abilities are valued, not just on one small project, but on projects to come.

For the truck driver, that moment came when he heard something he probably never imagined hearing: "Thank you. Because of what you did, you saved a life today."

In this case, Patricia's mother, because she worked in the training group of the trucking company, knew how the driver was supposed to respond based on the situation. So she could appreciate the driver's actions in a different and deeper way than even her daughter could.

Consider other examples demonstrating why appreciation is such a powerful influencer of great work.

Kelly, a journalist, reminisced how, during her second week on the job at a newspaper in Minnesota, a senior reporter received a standing ovation as he entered the newsroom. Apparently, the reporter was the first in the market to uncover a big story with exclusive interviews. Ever since that day, Kelly confided, she had sought the same response.

Picture, for a second, a crowd at a comedy club, booing a comedian off stage—probably one of the most painful visuals you can imagine. The comedian's intentions are good—to make people laugh. The crowd's intentions are to be entertained. Imagine this situation happening over and over again, each time making it harder to stand in front of the next spotlight. There's not a lot of great work or appreciation being shared, until the night a guy named Rodney Dangerfield, one of the more famous comedians of his time, sees something special in you—a unique talent.[6]

That's what happened to Jim Carrey, who, after witnessing his father lose his stable job in the insurance industry, vowed to become what his father had always dreamed of becoming—a comedian. Dangerfield, seeing something special, gave Carrey the chance to be his opening act, and not long after, Jim's career launched into stardom—all because the right person appreciated his talent. In a recent speech given to college graduates, Carrey relayed lessons he's learned throughout his life and career. Possibly the most profound statement he made was, "I can tell you that the effect you have on others is the most valuable currency there is."[7]

Most of us are not even aware of the impact we have on our team members. We talked to Bridgette, who is an electronics buyer for Best Buy. She received a letter from a former intern that had worked with her nearly ten years ago. "She told me I was the first person to truly believe in her. Honestly, I don't remember doing or saying anything special. I did not realize at the time the impact and influence I had on her—or probably all of the people I worked with throughout the years. I do, however, remember this intern specifically and thinking that she will be successful someday. I still have the card and letter she sent me. It meant a lot to discover that I had that much influence on her."

As a manager, consider how instances of appreciation could influence the future of great work from your team members. They're not just mere niceties or compliments. Thinking about ways you could show appreciation to your team might make you question whether or not your words and appreciation could have the same impact and influence as the words shared with you. We all question ourselves. But, again, reflect on your great work moments where you remember the person who influenced your work.

> ### Ask yourself these questions:
>
> - Who was the influencer?
> - What did they say or do?
> - What were the results that followed?

Detailing these moments in your life can instantly take you back. You may even experience the flutter or pride or excitement you felt. And you may ask yourself, "Why was that so powerful?"

AREN'T PEOPLE APPRECIATED ENOUGH?

If appreciation is so important, you would think that most leaders are adequately expressing it. But the truth is they're not. According to the O.C. Tanner Institute's 2016 Great Work Index research, one in four employees, globally, doesn't feel as if they are appreciated.[8] That number doesn't sound all that bad, does it? Nevertheless, realize that number accounts for all titles and levels within an organization—individual contributors, managers, directors, and all the way up the ladder. The point is if you hear that 75% of employees feel appreciated, you'd assume most companies are doing a good job of recognizing people. But there's a lot more to the story.

Here's where the numbers change drastically and can truly affect your role and ability as a leader. Notice in the chart below the significant drop in the number of non-manager, individual contributors who received recognition at work within the past month, compared to managers and above. As you can clearly see, recognition is not being given equally to all titles and roles. Individual contributors, by far, feel they receive the least recognition. And, in most companies, individual contributors are the bulk of the workforce.

Thinking specifically about the past month, which of the following best describes how often you have received recognition at work? —Often/Always

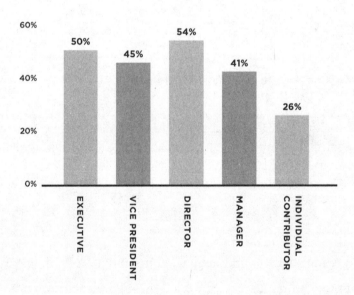

Think about how these responses might reflect your organization. Are the people leading the organization receiving the most praise for their work? And what does that low percentage, only 26%, mean when it comes to producing results for your team or organization? As

a leader in your company, this is your opportunity to influence results of the individual contributors. It's your opportunity to show them how much their work is appreciated, and it's your job to express your appreciation through recognition.

WHAT'S THE DIFFERENCE BETWEEN APPRECIATION AND RECOGNITION?

Although the words recognition and appreciation are often used interchangeably, there's a significant difference between them.

Appreciation is defined as the application of wisdom, sound judgment, and keen insight in recognizing the worth of someone. It is an emotion that is felt and unable to be faked.

Recognition is defined as the action or process of recognizing or being recognized, in particular. It is the act of using words to express gratitude.

A person's efforts and achievements must be appreciated, and that appreciation must be expressed through recognition if we want to influence great work. In summary, appreciation or the lack thereof, without question, has played a significant role in all our lives—both on the surface and on a deeply human level. You have experienced the impact and influence appreciation has had in your life and career. And consider the research that demonstrates appreciation for your work is not something you alone have experienced or desire. Appreciation is the one thing that influences everything else, and it's the number one thing employees at all levels and in all industries say will cause them to do great work. All of these statements are powerful if you learn to apply them to your life and work.

As a leader, you have the ability to influence others to create great work just as others have influenced you. So where do you start? What do you do? And will you be as influential as we say you will? Will you be as influential as the research shows you can be?

In the chapters that follow, you'll gain a new understanding of your role as a leader and learn how to create moments for others that inspire them to achieve results.

QUICK TAKE

Appreciation Influences Results

Appreciation is a powerful influencer of engagement, innovation, productivity, and business results.

There Is a Difference Between Appreciation and Recognition

Appreciation means to apply wisdom, sound judgment, and keen insight in recognizing the worth of someone. This is a deep human emotion. It is unable to be faked.

Recognition is the act of expressing appreciation.

To influence great work, appreciation is communicated through recognition.

CHAPTER 3

THE WORK OF A LEADER

After eighteen consecutive successful seasons, the Los Angeles Lakers did not make it into the 1993–94 playoffs. The winning streak had ended. The glory was gone. Ironically, many people pointed the finger of blame at the man who had taken the team to the playoffs so many times before as a player, the Lakers' new head coach, Earvin "Magic" Johnson.

Considered by some as the best point guard ever and deemed by the National Basketball Association as one of the fifty greatest players in history, Magic Johnson was admired and respected by everyone.[1] He was considered a voice of authority on the team. However, one and a half years after Johnson announced his retirement as a player and took the reigns as the Lakers' head coach, the so-called magic seemed to disappear. Johnson had failed as a manager. Why?

Sports analysts have picked and prodded into Johnson's short-lived, lackluster 1993–94 season as the Lakers' head coach (five wins and eleven losses).[2] Some blame generational differences between teammates. Others suggest that Magic himself could not connect with the younger guys or the team veterans. Whatever the reason, after sixteen-games as coach, Johnson vowed never to coach again. Somehow, even he knew that just because you have achieved personal greatness as a player, it does not mean you are automatically good at leading others to greatness.

A recent Gallup poll shows how wrong our assumptions can be when promoting people to leadership positions. The research found that the two most common reasons employees get promoted are, first, tenure, and second, success as a solo performer—neither of which, according to the study, indicate whether a person has the right skills to succeed as a leader. In fact, Gallup also reports that organizations make the mistake of hiring managers based on these criteria a whopping 82% of the time and that only one in ten people promoted to management positions naturally possess the talent to lead.[3]

It seems logical that when people are good at doing something—when they produce great results—they should get promoted to leadership positions. They should morph from contributors into leaders because our assumption is that people, like Magic Johnson, who create results surely can influence others to do the same.

Consider why you were promoted to your position. Most likely you showed proficiency in creating significant individual results. Most likely you were a great contributor.

Now, as a leader, think about your most common frustrations surrounding the people who work on your team. Maybe you find yourself thinking, "Why do I still have to get involved to get the results we need?" Or maybe you wonder, "Don't these people want to do great work? Why aren't they putting their full effort into it?" All of these are common complaints we hear from the many thousands of managers we interview through surveys, polls, and face-to-face interviews.

If you struggle with any of these common management thoughts, it may actually be you who needs to reset your thinking, not your team members.

MINDSET 1: TRANSITION FROM CONTRIBUTOR TO INFLUENCER

Your role has changed as a leader of people. Yes, your job is still to create results, but instead of producing the results yourself, your responsibility is to learn how to influence the results of your team.

Let's look at another team record coming to an end after fifteen years, when Alex Ferguson ended a losing streak for Aberdeen to win the Scottish Football League Championship. Ferguson, like Johnson, became a coach not long after announcing his retirement as a player. On the field, he was good, a leader. However, as a player, he was not at the same level as Magic Johnson was on the court.

Nevertheless, Ferguson's leadership blossomed from the sidelines as a manager. Sure, he, too, stumbled through his first years managing a team rather than playing for one. However, by the time he retired as team manager of Manchester United from 1986 to 2013, Ferguson is regarded by players, managers, and analysts to be the greatest football manager of all time—honing and developing players like Paul Scholes, Ryan Giggs, Eric Cantona, David Beckham, and Cristiano Ronaldo. "The job of a manager," commented Ferguson, ". . . like that of a teacher, is to inspire people to be better. Give them better technical skills, make them winners, make them better people, and they can go anywhere in life."[4]

Knighted by Queen Elizabeth II, Sir Alex Ferguson today is recognized for his leadership ability on the sidelines. On the other hand, Magic Johnson, a few years after trying his hand at coaching, went back into the locker room in 1996 and played another thirty-two games for the Los Angeles Lakers. Both men are leaders in their own right. However, it was Ferguson who was able to reset his thinking and influence others to greatness—inspiring them, teaching them, and leading them to victory as a manager.

A simple shift in thinking, or a profound reset in your mind, is what separates good leaders from marginal managers. It separates those who have the ability to lead others to greatness and those who simply meet expectations. Former CEO of General Electric, Jack Welch, may have best clarified this reset when he said, "Before you are a leader, success is all about growing yourself. When you become a leader, success is all about growing others."[5]

HOW DO YOU INFLUENCE PEOPLE?

Leading as a contributor versus as a leader requires two completely different approaches. While a top performer will certainly have an influence from time to time, a leader's real role and focus are entirely about influencing others. The role of a leader is to achieve results through the great work of others. In Magic Johnson's case, setting an example of gameplay was not enough. He needed to make the transition.

Leaders are not just role models, although they probably were great role models as individual contributors. However, if they do not make the transition from contributor to leader and understand they influence others either positively or negatively from the sidelines, they will not be great leaders.

Research conducted and published by management consultants Jack Zenger and Joseph Folkman clearly illustrates the effect and influence of both good and bad leaders. Their research shows a trickle-down effect of both good and bad leadership and how both become more pronounced based on the effectiveness of the highest-level leader.[6]

To see how both good and bad managers affected their direct reports and the ability of those direct reports to lead others, Zenger and Folkman examined 360-degree assessments of high-level leaders and of their direct reports who were mid-level managers. They matched 265 pairs of senior leaders and their mid-level-manager direct reports and found interesting correlations of behaviors. In a nutshell, good and bad leadership does not end with a direct report. In fact, some of the behaviors that had the highest correlations (that seemed to trickle down the most, almost as if they were contagious) were:

Developing self and others	**Consideration and cooperation**
Technical skills	**Integrity and honesty**
Strategy skills	**Results focus**

It is important, however, when reading the above list to consider that these leadership behaviors were displayed by mid-level managers as prominently, if not more prominently, than they were shown by senior leaders. If a senior leader was deemed highly effective in a particular area, so was that manager's direct report.

"In plain terms," explained the researchers, "... that means if you are a high-level manager doing a subpar job, you erode not only the engagement of those working for you but also the engagement of the people working for them." And the opposite is true as well. If you are doing a superb job as a manager, you will elevate the engagement of all those who report up to you.

WHY SHOULD YOU MANAGE DIFFERENTLY?

Lizzie, a senior manager at an engineering firm in Sydney, Australia, informed us she rejected numerous promotions to leadership positions within her former organization because, she said, "I believed the role of the manager was to control, police, and manipulate people." It was not until she left that company after seventeen years before she understood the positive impact she could have on others. "I had never met a manager that inspired me to be better."

As simple as it may sound, Lizzie is much like many other people when they are first asked to lead. Again, they were great contributors. They were excellent at achieving results. And, although it is a compliment to be called upon to lead, it is human nature to view the role of management through your experiences of being managed.

How do you treat people? How do you create results through others, whether they report to you or not? How do you leverage other people's time, talent, and ability? Moreover, what causes so many of us to default to a command-and-control model of leadership rather than a style that inspires and influences people to greatness?

The answer is relatively straightforward: we must begin by resetting the way we think. We must realize that just because we are good at creating results in our way, others will be good at creating results in their way. Other players on the Los Angeles Lakers could not be Magic Johnson. They needed to be inspired to be themselves. They needed coaching and plays that allowed their unique abilities to grow and thrive. They needed to be inspired to become the best version of themselves, not the next-best version of Magic.

"Studies on control and influence in autocratic, democratic, and laissez-faire organizations show the most effective organizations have teams where everyone feels he or she has influence," added Joe Folkman about the trickle-down effect of leadership. "When people feel like their voice is heard, their investment in their work increases far more than when they are being told what to do and exactly how to do it."[7]

To reset your mindset:

- Look closely at your team members' unique skills and abilities instead of trying to get them to mimic your or others' unique talents and abilities.

- Invite ideas, personal expression, and a sense of shared ownership into projects and practices so team members understand how they can make an impact.

- Help break down and remove obstacles that may hinder someone from contributing their best work.

MINDSET 2: YOUR TEAM WANTS TO MAKE A DIFFERENCE

It is an old-school but still common assumption that a manager's role is to keep their team in line, keep up productivity, and correct the mistakes of those who seemingly know little about how to do their job. Somewhere, probably during the industrial revolution, an assumption also arose that unless employees were "managed" into giving effort nothing would get done. No matter how dated these assumptions may be, many leaders still operate under these notions as if there is nothing they can do about it.

However, there is something you can do. It is not managing with tighter restraint. It is not employee surveillance or more stringent policy creation. It is not more rules. In fact, the thing that needs to be reset is your thinking—toward a notion that people come to work wanting to make a difference, wanting to add value, and wanting to create meaningful results. The simple truth is this: what you believe about people significantly expands your influence.

Think of yourself at the doorstep of your current job on your first day. Did you show up wanting to be marginal? Did you show up lacking in excitement and enthusiasm? Did you turn up thinking you were being hired to fly under the radar and that you would just work hard enough not to get disciplined? Did you show up believing that you were entirely dependent on a manager to get your best work out of you? No. Most likely, you were thrilled the company chose you over all the other candidates for your unique abilities. You were ready to bring your talent, exert your full energy, and draw upon all your previous experience to do a great job. The same applies to those on your team. They wanted to come into their job and shine. They have dreams and aspirations and hopes to make a difference, just as you do.

"Early in my leadership journey, I worked for Costco," Sheldon said. "That is where I made a huge mistake and learned one of the most valuable lessons in my leadership career."

These are the words of Sheldon Harris, former CEO of Cold Stone Creamery from 1996 to 2006, a company that catapulted from just a handful of corner ice cream stores to more than 1,400 world-wide locations under Harris's leadership.

We met a few times with Sheldon while conducting research for this book. He has been an employee. He has been a manager.

He has been a high-profile CEO. Today Sheldon is a partner at CEO Coaching International, an organization that trains the world's top entrepreneurs and CEOs on how to accelerate their businesses and lead people. Sheldon could share many stories and observations about leading people. However, one story he told us clarified just how important this seemingly simple practice can be and how it can turn horribly wrong.

"Back then, during my stint at Costco, I held the position of Front End Manager, which meant that I was responsible for all of the employees working in the front area of the building, including the cashiers, boxers, cart collectors, and entry door security. I will never forget an incident with a newly hired employee. His name was Tim. Costco had a company policy that three occurrences of tardiness within a thirty-day period would result in a written warning. Shortly after Tim was hired, I noticed that he clocked in late for his shift. Of course, I documented it, just like I had been trained."

Sheldon explained that, at the time, his perception of managing people was to ensure that mistakes were not being made. And, he confessed, after witnessing the first incident with Tim's tardiness, he began paying close attention to the clock.

"I was watching for another infraction," said Sheldon. "And it did not take long before Tim received three strikes." Harris remembers thinking, "I got him."

Just as the company policy stated, Sheldon wrote up a formal disciplinary notice and sat down with Tim to present it.

"Tim did not deny the tardiness," Sheldon related. "There wasn't any sign of guilt on Tim's face."

Squirming with a gut feeling he was punishing Tim without good reason, Sheldon recounted that the young man finally interjected. "Aren't you going to ask why I clocked in late?"

"That is a question I, as a young leader, should have considered," said Sheldon, still shaking his head in disbelief. "But now I am in a room with this guy, I have created conflict, and I have potentially already built a relationship of mistrust with a new employee."

After a long, anguishing pause, Sheldon finally asked, "Why did you clock in late?"

"I saw you picking up trash and cardboard in the parking lot every day when you were on your way into the building," replied Tim. "I assumed that if it was important enough for you to do, then I should do it too."

"I had made a huge mistake," said Sheldon. "This guy was applying his discretionary effort which should be applauded. And there I was, making accusations and preparing to discipline him for the situation. It was a big lesson for me as a leader. We need to notice the real efforts of people. And we need to applaud them when we understand that their intentions are to improve the business."[8]

Like Sheldon, many managers falsely believe their job is to seek out mistakes and make corrections—to look for the negative, the struggling, or those who are not creating wins for the company. However, this foot-in-mouth situation helped Sheldon reset his thinking and the way he thought about how his employees approached their work.

WHAT HAPPENS WHEN LEADERS BELIEVE THEIR TEAM
MEMBERS WANT TO MAKE A DIFFERENCE?

As described earlier, Zenger and Folkman's research showed how both good and bad leadership makes its way into the culture of organizations. Additionally, the leaders' belief systems also have a profound effect on those they lead. If senior-level leaders believe employees are showing up at work to make a difference, so will mid-level leaders, employees, and, in the following example, even former employees.

Ten years ago Jubilant FoodWorks Ltd., the exclusive Domino's Pizza franchisee in India, was, in a nutshell, failing. They were bleeding red ink and struggling to service their debt. Under these difficult circumstances, they wanted to give the company one more shot, under the guidance of a new CEO.

Stepping into the chief executive officer role of a failing organization was not exactly the dream job Ajay Kaul had anticipated for his next career move. Ajay had no experience in the food industry—none. Earning the respect of the 3,000 employees he was about to lead probably seemed as implausible as handling the food hygiene problems in a country with poor roads, terrible traffic, and unpredictable delivery times.

Was it marketing that was making the company fail? Operations? Was it a lack of service or product quality? It is easy to assume the "harder" aspects of business would be the first on the list of things to change within the company. However, Ajay chose to focus on "the emotional connection between his people, their customers, and their brand." Fundamentally, he wanted his people to believe they had the power to create change. That may sound like a risky move for a guy stepping into an industry where he had no experience. However, employees rallied around the new (even seemingly whimsical at first glance) mission: "We bring happiness into your household."

Think about that. After years of focusing on speed, accuracy, and efficiency, this new mission challenged employees to create an emotional outcome from their work—happiness. This mission accomplished much more than creating a fresh perspective on what they did. It placed an important focus on each employee making a difference for their customers. It set a high bar, one that signaled to every employee that happiness was valued in the workplace. It also showed the leader believed all employees were capable of fulfilling a big mission—to deliver happiness instead of only delivering pizza. It invited everyone to join in.

Next, Ajay did something that showed his people he believed in their intentions at work and that he was there to support them. Ajay made his personal cell number available to all employees. While CEOs of most large companies typically try to maintain some protective distance from their people, Ajay wanted every employee to have his number because, in his words, "I want them to have the peace of mind that they can call the CEO in the moment of distress."

Think about what giving your personal cell number out to your entire staff communicates. It says, "I trust you. I believe you will make the right decision, and if something arises, I am always here to support you." This also serves as a powerful reminder that every voice has a way of being heard by the CEO. Also note, Ajay receives few calls from his employees because they're empowered to solve their issues without him.

Ajay chose to send another clear message to his leadership team about who was serving whom. He insists that every leader go out and work at one of the stores each quarter. He says it "brings them straight into the moment of truth with customers." It also gives him insights from employees about what is on their minds. Perhaps bigger than that, he stated, is it sends a clear message that every single job is important. It brings dignity and respect to every individual whether they "make it, bake it, or deliver it."

Every quarter senior leaders' bonuses are based on the survey scores of the store managers. Since the stores are the profit centers of the company, Ajay feels corporate leaders' value should be deter-mined by them—how supportive they are and how much value they create for the stores. Not the other way around.

Ajay's trust and belief in his team worked. Today, instead of sharing his cell phone number with 3,000 employees, he shares it with 28,000. India is the second largest Domino's market outside the United States. The franchise reports an astounding 70% market share in India. They make more than 55 million deliveries each year, with an equal number of customers ordering via carryout.

The impact Ajay had was born of his belief in his people. He had a sense they wanted to be part of a greater cause and wanted to do more than produce and deliver pizza. They wanted to make a difference for their customers. Something they could be proud of, something that brought out their best work.

Ajay is clearly proud of his team and what they have accomplished. Their shared success is now fully part of their culture. However, even he was surprised by how that culture has extended beyond their employees.

While bringing in the New Year, millions of families in India now choose to celebrate with pizza. On December 31, the CEO, his leadership team, and every employee report for duty at Domino's Pizza stores throughout the country. It is their busiest day of the year, so it is an all-hands-on-deck effort to keep up with demand. On New Year's Eve 2014, their employees were joined by more than 1,000 *former* employees who volunteered to help deliver happiness to Domino's customers that night. The sense of connection and appreciation shared within the organization had become so powerful that it inspired people to work *for free* to help their former colleagues.

Ajay reset the thinking at Domino's by acknowledging that people want to make a difference and believing they can make that difference. He showed them he believed in their ability to deliver on the promise. He showed them he trusted them, appreciated their ability and effort, and why their ability and effort was important.[9]

NOT MY PEOPLE. MY PEOPLE ARE DIFFERENT.

As we interview and interact with leaders around the world, inevitably someone will tell us how different, even unmotivated or disengaged their people are at work. They will say, "I agree with these leadership principles, but you have not met my team. I cannot get them to move an inch for the company if they don't get paid more or reprimanded."

However much we would like to believe these naysayers are being honest, we have seen the evidence that people want to do great things at work too many times to believe there is a statistically relevant exception to the rule. It is much like discussing heart disease as the number one killer in America but assuming nobody you know will die of it. Sure, everybody can name one exception to the rule—Great Uncle Eddie smoked three packs a day, ate donuts for dinner, and lived to be ninety-seven years old—but it is rare.

Extensive global research shows that people who produce great results begin with the intention of making a difference—they want their work to be appreciated, add value, and create an impact. One such body of research, the Great Work Study conducted by the O.C. Tanner Institute, analyzed a random sample of 10,000 cases of award-winning work throughout various industries, regions around the world, and within all levels of organizations. It revealed that when an employee approaches their work with a simple, focused intention—to create a difference other people would love—they end up doing just that.[10]

Most people want to be successful. Most people want to achieve great things—to grow, develop and create a difference in their team or organization that is valued and appreciated. It is an undeniable trait of humanity. However, it does make you wonder: If everyone wants to, why isn't everyone doing great work?

The answer to that question is not all that complicated. We have found through research, interviews, and analysis that the simple answer is this: If people are not doing great work, it is usually because of how they are being led. Every one of us has seen the engaging influence of a great leader. We have watched how a leader can come into an underperforming team and, within a matter of weeks or months, that same team rallies and excels. Somehow all the talent and ingredients for success were there all along. The leader did something to bring the team alive.

The *USS Benfold* might be the perfect example. The destroyer ship was, at one time, the worst-performing ship in the United States Navy suffering from low morale, inflated operating expenses, and poor safety standards. Few thought this ship could improve. Enter Naval Commander Mike Abrashoff, tasked with transforming the ship's lackluster performance using the same crew of 310 sailors.

Of course, the captain quickly saw multiple problems that he faced as the ship's new leader. But, he also saw the issues were related. For example, let's focus on just the safety issues on the *USS Benfold*. It may seem a little ironic to discuss safety concerns on something that is inherently unsafe—a destroyer ship. However, when thirty-one sailors were directly involved with some injury-producing mishap, it was evident there was a problem. This problem had little to do with clumsiness. And it had little to do with policy, as most policies are shared across the entire Naval fleet. No, this was a problem with culture; the sailors were not safe because their superiors were not engaging them in safety concerns.

Abrashoff, instead of just commanding that sailors become safer, decided he would specifically focus on one of the *USS Benfold's* twenty-four teams each week. He would talk to sailors, he would inspect their workspaces, and he would ask them questions about safety, process, and concerns.

As you might imagine, having the captain come hang out for the week and express his caring and concern would feel like an honor and probably make a significant impact on what the sailors saw as important.

After twelve months and many conversations, the *USS Benfold* became the highest performing ship, when it came to safety, in the

United States Navy. In fact, a year later, the ship reported just two minor incidents, which Captain Abrashoff still claimed to be, "Two too many."

Safety wasn't the issue, culture was. Personnel turnover also decreased to an unprecedented 1%, the rate of military promotions tripled, and the crew slashed operating expenses by 25%.

Just one thing changed on the *USS Benfold*—one perception, that was held by just one person. Although this story might sound like an unlikely circumstance, the point of the story is not just to compliment the leadership of the captain, but instead, it is to shine a spotlight on the fact that the sailors wanted to be safe and responded quickly to one small change.[11]

In the state of California is a place called Death Valley, one of the hottest, driest places on earth. It only rains about two inches per year. However, in the winter of 2015, more than seven inches of rain fell on the parched and barren desert sands, something that had not happened in many years.

In the spring of 2016, something remarkable happened. Spring flowers covered the entire floor of Death Valley. Within days, photographers, botanists, and tourists traveled from across America, and from other regions of the world, to see the impossible become possible. In fact, the circumstances were so rare that those who were able to witness what experts call a "superbloom" may never again see such a circumstance in their lifetime. Overnight, Death Valley was alive with fresh, vibrant growth—5,270 square miles of bright yellow, purple and pink wildflowers painting the typically monotone desert floor.

"If you get the chance to see a bloom in Death Valley, especially a superbloom, you should take the opportunity to see it because it could be a once-in-a-lifetime opportunity," counseled Park Ranger Alan Van Valkenburg. ". . . There are so many seeds out there, just waiting to sprout, just waiting to grow. I had no idea that there was that much out there. When you get the perfect conditions, the perfect storm so to speak, those seeds can all sprout at once."[12]

What this proved, of course, was that Death Valley was not dead at all. Instead, it was dormant—probably like a lot of those people who have not fully engaged in their work. The desert was merely waiting for the proper conditions. When the conditions were right, life, beauty, color, and excitement flourished.

Waiting for people to engage without giving them a reason to engage is much like waiting for flowers to grow without water. This example of Death Valley raises these questions that are important to ask yourself about your leadership style and your team environment.

Ask yourself:

- Can you reset your thinking to give people the opportunity to do things you never imagined they could accomplish?

- Are you creating the kind of environment and conditions that allow people to do great work?

- What is missing (what's your version of rain on the desert) that could help your team thrive?

In your own workplace, you cannot make a flower bloom, but you can provide the right conditions to make it possible. The same is true with people. The Great Work Index suggests that while 86% of employees want to do great work (feel like it is their responsibility), only 63% feel they actually can.[13] Though you may not be able to command people to greatness, your responsibility as a leader is to provide the right conditions and leadership influence to inspire it.

QUICK TAKE

There are two mindset shifts that must happen to effectively become a leader of people:

Transition from a Contributor to an Influencer

Influencers see people for their unique skills and abilities. They invite ideas and provide a sense of ownership and expression which allows people a personal opportunity to make an impact. They also eliminate boundaries so their team can do their personal best.

Trust that People Inherently Want to Make a Difference

Influencing people does not mean policing people; it means believing employees came to make a difference. It means people have talents they want to use, hone, and improve so they can become their best. It means people want to be trusted, cheered for, and recognized for what they offer to the team.

Though you may not be able to command people to greatness, your responsibility as a leader is to provide the right conditions and leadership influence to inspire it.

CHAPTER 4

HOW AND WHAT DO YOU APPRECIATE?

In less than fifteen minutes, a psychologist can observe a married couple's micro expressions (brief, involuntary facial expressions) on film and predict their potential for divorce with more than 90% accuracy. This is according to research that began in the early 1980s by psychologist John Gottman.

In this research, Gottman hypothesized that a ratio of five positive responses to one negative response would predict a successful relationship.[1] In 1992, the researcher teamed up with two mathematicians to test this hypothesis. Recruiting 700 couples who had just received a marriage certificate, researchers filmed a fifteen-minute conversation between a husband and wife and counted the number of positive and negative micro expressions. Then, using that five-to-one ratio, they placed their bets on whether or not those couples would last.

Ten years passed. The researchers contacted the couples in the study to see if their predictions were correct. They were. The team predicted divorce with 94% accuracy.[2]

We wondered, if tiny expressions can mean so much to a relationship, then how big of an impact could intentional verbal expressions have—when communication is clear, purposeful, and meaningful to that relationship?

It is short-sighted to assume that any form of non-verbal communication will adequately communicate your appreciation to an employee. A smile, head nod, or even a thumbs up can't possibly express your positive thoughts, just as a frown, head-shake, or thumbs down couldn't possibly communicate a correction that is needed in an employee's behavior. Consider the following sayings and the difference between what the leader is saying and what the employee might be hearing.

NEGATIVE MESSAGES	
Words Spoken By Leader	**Message Received By Employee**
You were not late today, were you?	My leader does not know what I do.
If you have something important to say...	My thoughts are not valued.
Can I trust you?	Why was I hired?
Just don't mess it up...	I am expendable.
... (nothing)...	They do not like me.

POSITIVE MESSAGES	
Words Spoken By Leader	**Message Received By Employee**
Great job on that presentation.	My leader notices what I do.
You are talented.	I am unique and valued for being me.
If anyone can do it, it is you.	My leader believes in me.
Thank you for all your great work over the past three years.	I am committed and like it here.
Thanks for staying late to get that out...	They appreciate the fact that I care.

Notice how, especially in the negative messages, the intention of the leader may not be suggesting (at all) what the employee believes is being communicated. The employee interprets the communication and makes assumptions about what the leader is saying. The employee makes assumptions about the connection they have to their leader, their work, and the organization, depending on how they interpret the message. The employee may even assume, due to the words chosen or left unspoken, that their leader does not like the way they do their job. They might also make incorrect assumptions about their connection to the organization—that they are simply working there, rather than being an integral part of it.

It is easy to read the previous statements and see how they could be miscommunicated. It is easy to see how a lack of communication could cause anxiety in an employee's mind. We have heard stories of employees leaving organizations due to a lack of appreciation, and we have heard from employers who were shocked to find out these employees felt such a disconnect. "I ran into an employee at an industry event a few years after he left," recounted Margaret, a manager at an auto dealership. "I told him how much we missed him and that we had struggled to find someone that could match his passion and skill." Margaret paused. "Do you know how he responded?" she asked, seeming almost embarrassed. "He looked surprised and replied, 'I wish you would have told me that when I worked for you.'"

The words we choose or choose not to use have a dramatic impact on people. They can influence people to become their best, but they can also influence people to perform marginally, or even poorly, because employees are not being told what is truly appreciated.

WHAT DO YOU APPRECIATE?

Books, music, movies, restaurants, and yes, the way we work are all valued in different ways by different people. Still, one of the questions we hear most is "What should I recognize people for?"

Our response has always been to recognize people for the actions, ideas, and results that you as a leader value most, and for the things that align that employee's work with the mission, vision, and values of the organization. That is the simple answer.

Research and analysis we conducted on thousands of examples of award-winning work revealed, however, that there are certain things that get recognized and that leaders appreciate more than others—actions, ideas, and efforts that create results.

Consider the experience of Pari, a housekeeping manager at a hotel in Singapore. Her staff was responsible for alerting the food and beverage group when the in-room coffee makers were running low on coffee so they could restock them. A housekeeper on her team made an insightful observation: "We already bring drinking glasses and bottled water to each room. Why shouldn't we carry coffee packets on our carts too? Why should the guest have to wait for us to contact the beverage group?" The idea was quickly implemented. Pari recognized that employee publicly for questioning and improving an old process. "She saved the food and beverage group time. It is better for the guests as well."

Another common thing leaders recognize people for is giving extra effort. Dylan from Detroit, Michigan, and his team had worked hard on a high-stakes sales presentation. They knew their little company was the underdog, as their competition had far more resources. But they resolved to give it their all anyway.

The night before the presentation, a massive snowstorm hit Detroit. All flights were grounded. Dylan knew his odds of making it out on the early flight to Chicago were slim because the storm was supposed to get worse. So Dylan jumped in his car and drove seven and a half hours through the blowing snow (typically a four-to six-hour drive) to make the presentation.

Dylan's manager was so impressed by his commitment that he publicly recognized Dylan at the next company meeting. And, by the way, the client heard that Dylan had driven through the storm as well. They gave that little persistent company a chance.

Going the extra mile, not settling for an expected outcome, challenging old processes, gaining insight from external sources, and improving their work product are common things leaders from around the world seem to appreciate most. Simply stated, leaders appreciate great work—work that achieves a result that is appreciated, valued, and recognized by someone else, whether it be a coworker, a customer, or a leader. Great work leads to better-than-expected outcomes.

What is great work on your team?

Raley's Supermarkets, based in California, is one of those companies that sets the standard in a competitive grocery store industry. The company is committed to serving its customers, but it also understands the importance of helping its employees do their best work.

We had an interesting meeting with Mark Foley, Senior Vice President of Human Resources and Labor Relations at Raley's. We were talking about how appreciation, if done purposefully, not only improves engagement but enhances the quality of work when Mark asked an insightful question: "Who determines what great work is?"

In the discussion that ensued, Mark discussed the importance of reinforcing actions that aligned at Raley's. We talked about how leaders must learn to identify and recognize the particular work that is vital to the team achieving their objectives. We pointed out that the leader is in the best position to purposefully define what great work looks like for their team. In the case of Raley's Supermarkets, it was the store managers who could best determine what actions to recognize that would most impact the customer experience.

Of course, the details of what a supermarket store manager should recognize are entirely different from a foreman of a construction crew. A sales manager must recognize different qualities than someone who works in a tax attorney's office. Still, many of the actions leaders recognize are similar, no matter their industry. In spite of this fact, many people remain in the dark when it comes to understanding their leaders' expectations regarding what constitutes great work.

Lorna, a marketing writer for an auto parts retailer, had worked for a company for eleven years. She did her job. She met her deadlines. And, although her office was across the hall from the CEO's office, he never spoke to her. "I did not think he knew my name," she recalled, ". . . until the seventh year of my employment."

Lorna recounted that her direct supervisor was good at recognizing her when he thought something she wrote was good. "I never really had a sense of what the CEO wanted, though. My manager was good at telling me what he liked. However, there was always this gray area—almost like he was unsure from one piece to the next if we were producing marketing materials that the CEO liked."

Lorna enjoyed her job. She liked the environment and loved her co-workers but had been looking for a new job because there was always an uneasy question in her gut whether or not she was making a difference. "I loved what I did, but I was becoming frustrated by the fact that when I would try new things, and approach my work in different ways, I never knew if what I did was loved, overlooked, or hated. It is not just that I did not know that my work was appreciated, I also never received any negative feedback."

After seven years and minimal feedback, Lorna thought she would test the waters in hopes of generating a reaction. "I was ready to leave, which meant I was ready to be fired," she explained. "I had three fairly significant projects on my plate for the week. I completed one the way I normally would—solid content. The second one I took over the top with language. I used words that typically I would not write—sizzling language that quite honestly I thought sounded overly dramatic. For the third project, instead of writing sales copy, I wrote a poem to communicate the message. It was a humorous spin that we had never tried before. I knew my manager would feel uneasy about presenting the material, but I asked him to submit it anyway, saying I would take the blame if the CEO hated it."

Lorna was nervous the day her ideas were presented to the CEO. "I remember working in my cubicle and thinking that this might be my last day."

She heard the CEO's door open across the hallway. She could hear his footsteps—a fast clicking noise against the marble floor—as he made his way into her work group. "Can all of you stand?" requested the CEO as he entered.

"He was known for having a temper," said Lorna. "I recall all seven of us standing nervously."

"I know you all work hard," announced the CEO, "but this latest edition of our newsletter is, by far, the most interesting thing you have ever created. You all deserve kudos."

The CEO then went into her manager's office and closed the door. "I hoped it was one of my pieces that had made him pay attention," Lorna confided. "But I wasn't sure. I didn't know what everyone else on the team had submitted to that newsletter. Maybe he loved my stuff. Or perhaps it was someone else's work that he was referring to."

Again, Lorna heard her manager's door open and the CEO's footsteps clicking across the floor. She nearly jumped out of her chair when a hand landed firmly on her shoulder. "Lorna, I loved the fact that you are willing to try new things. We need more of that. We need to be trying new approaches in every newsletter. I don't know if the readers will like it, but I love it."

Lorna stayed with the company four more years—she called them the best four years of her career. The CEO's appreciation had communicated to her exactly what was expected of her. It was not to be perfect. It was not to be consistent. It was to try new creative approaches. For Lorna to do great work, she needed to know and understand what the CEO valued.

WHAT IS GOING TO MAKE THE BIGGEST IMPACT ON YOUR TEAM'S RESULTS?

The reason appreciation has a higher impact than all other influencers of great work is because it communicates in the sincerest and most authentic way what is valued. As a leader, it is important to know the answer to this question: What are the things you value that contribute to your team's results?

Gary discovered what was valued by his leader while working at Frito-Lay. "I was assigned to the Doritos brand, and I was relatively new to the organization," he said. "I recall sitting in a meeting with my team and our agency and reviewing a thirty-second television ad. Our job was to decide between three alternative endings to the ad, and I disagreed with everyone. All the senior members liked one version, but I thought another version was better. I specifically recall my leader asking if everyone agreed and looked around the room to see if anyone spoke up. No one did. If no one else was going to say anything, I felt I had to speak up no matter what the consequences. I was a little scared, to be honest. It was the first time I spoke my mind."

The next day, Gary was surprised when his manager gathered the entire team to publicly recognize him. "I want to recognize Gary because he disagreed with me," she said. She then continued to express how she, and the company, valued the opinions of every employee and how important it is that everyone speak their mind.

"That set a precedent for me," declared Gary. "It made me confident to express my opinion and encourage others to express their opinions, because those differences in opinion lead to better decisions and outcomes. It's a lesson that has changed the way I interact and think today."

The leader's recognition of Gary spoke volumes about what she valued and expected from all employees. And it is an excellent example of taking advantage of a naturally occurring situation and turning it into a moment of appreciation.

BECOMING A CONNOISSEUR OF GREAT WORK

Like a connoisseur, foodie, art aficionado, or movie buff, it is your job as a leader to gain a heightened awareness of great work. It takes a sensitivity and a level of discernment to know the value of great work performed by your team members. It is less about looking for mistakes and more about having an eye for brilliance, action, innovation, and effort. It is your job to tune in to the levers that create results. You have seen the connoisseurs, the aficionados, and critics in action. They can

see and call out things the rest of us have not paid attention to before—
the hint of a smoky flavor in wine, the color simplicity of a piece of art,
or the richness of a masterfully produced scene that makes an entire
movie turn into a moving masterpiece.

Some time ago, Kevin had the opportunity to attend a basketball
game with former professional basketball player Rick Barry. "That is
not an opportunity you turn down," he asserted. "How often do you get
to watch a game with one of the best players of that game? What I did
not realize that evening was the education I would receive by sitting
with a guy who truly understands basketball. I have played basketball
my entire life. But sitting next to Rick as he analyzed movements
on the court—the way players moved and positioned themselves, or
how they anticipated their opponents' next steps—I realized I did not
appreciate basketball the way he did. He saw the game at an entirely
different level. His appreciation of the game caused me to appreciate
it with an entirely new and elevated perspective."

A group of us were attending a conference in Las Vegas, Nevada.
We decided to have dinner at Lotus of Siam, a Thai restaurant that
had earned numerous accolades.[3] After looking at the menu for just
a few minutes, David looked at the server and said, "Everything looks
so good. Why don't you bring us your favorites—enough for all of us at
the table. You choose."

The waiter, seemingly shocked, smiled. His excitement to share
his expertise was evident. Who would know the best dishes on the
menu better than him? He was the true connoisseur. His excitement
showed with every dish he brought to the table as he gave detailed
descriptions of what we were about to eat and why it was different
or better.

That dinner became more than just a meal. It became an experience, because we had invited the connoisseur to shine. And, we all agreed, it was the best Thai meal we have ever had.

Think about the people you know who would be considered connoisseurs in their chosen endeavor. Most likely a few people come to mind. Think about a person who may have a financial eye that is unreal. They can scan numbers and quickly spot when something is wrong in a statement or report. Or a sales representative who has an innate ability to read a room during a presentation and somehow pick up on unspoken concerns. The point is a well-trained eye has a sensitivity toward excellence, in any endeavor, that can pinpoint the smallest details that lead to the greatest results.

Being a connoisseur of great work means you have developed the sensitivity to know great work when you see it and to spot it in a heartbeat. And knowing how to show your appreciation through recognition allows you, the leader, to have the greatest amount of influence on your team's results. You have the opportunity to influence your team based on the specific things you value and your company values. It's a naturally occurring process that supports, inspires, and elevates people to the very reason they joined your company—because they wanted to make a difference. They want to create significant results. Every step that leads up to those results, well, that is what you want to recognize because that's what you naturally appreciate.

BECOMING A MASTER OF APPRECIATION

The following chapters will make it easy as we show you how to express your appreciation by acknowledging a handful of naturally occurring opportunities to effectively express your gratitude. In fact, the primary excuse we hear from managers who don't practice regular recognition is, "I don't have time." And, we will warn you now, 79% of people who leave jobs report "a lack of appreciation" as the reason they left. It is time to make time, and if you focus on these naturally occurring opportunities, you quickly realize that you have not only become a connoisseur of great work, but also a master of appreciation.

Fuel daily value-creating activities   Focus on outcomes to drive results

Sustain performance over a career

Opportunity #1: Encourage Effort

This is when you notice effort being applied toward a result that you or your organization values. Maybe the person applying the effort has not achieved the result yet, but the effort is apparent, and a little bit of cheering will help give them the inspiration to keep moving forward.

Opportunity #2: Reward Results

This is when a person or team achieves a result, big or small, that aligns with your team or company's priorities. Of course, results can vary in size and impact. It could be a small victory, big win, or a significant achievement.

Opportunity #3: Celebrate Careers

Our careers are the accumulation of our work. Celebrating a career milestone is an opportunity to show appreciation for a person's body of work and for the person as a whole. It's a celebration of achievements, life events, and value they bring to the team. It focuses on who they are and can include anything from their humor at work, the support they give their team, or the fascinating tales they tell at the lunch table about their weekend adventures.

We all need to hold ourselves accountable to express appreciation for the people who apply effort, achieve results, and commit their skills, talents, and ideas, to the purpose of the team or organization. But, remember, it is your job to influence results. You probably already made notes of the great work you can recognize immediately. However, don't jump in carelessly. Our research not only shows how important appreciation is when it comes to influencing great work, but it also reveals how to express your appreciation for the biggest impact, which makes the next three chapters critical. They share the actions and insights to help you become a connoisseur of great work and a master of appreciation.

QUICK TAKE

The words we choose or choose not to use have a dramatic impact on people. They can influence people to become their best or their worst. Appreciation should be shown for activities that align with your goals, the team's goals, and the company's goals. It should spotlight work that is relevant to the recipient of that work. It should also spotlight the goals of the recipient as they strive to become their best.

Three naturally occurring opportunities exist for appreciation:

Encourage Effort: When employees apply efforts that exceed expectations, are sustained, focused, and directed at a specific outcome, they deserve to be applauded, cheered for, and encouraged.

Reward Results: When employees produce positive outcomes, results, and acomplishments, they deserve to be rewarded because the employee has a made a difference that is valued, loved, and admired.

Celebrate Careers: When employees hit career milestones, a history of contributions—efforts, experiences, and ideas— deserve to be celebrated. People want a celebration that represents their effort, commitment, contribution, accomplishments, and connection to the company.

CHAPTER 5

ENCOURAGE EFFORT

Mike is a technical project manager that works for an advertising agency in Los Angeles. We heard about Mike from Josie, who told us this story about encouraging effort. She said her agency was brainstorming ideas to create a presentation for a luxury jet service. Almost the entire creative team was assigned to the project. In the boardroom were six creative employees—the creative director, a writer, two graphic designers, a web designer, and Mike. Mike was the guy who typically focused more on function, process, and print runs, rather than actual design. "The creative director in that meeting had only been with the company for a few weeks," said Josie. "He did not know us well. He was not well aware of our skill sets. And, although the owners of the agency had pigeon-holed us all quite well—I was the more feminine and fancy designer, Chuck was the manlier designer, Claire was the social media and web guru, and Mike was the function and process guy—our new creative director didn't seem to pay any attention to our traditional roles."

Josie said that after hours of conversation and ideas, Mike asked the creative director if he could leave the meeting because he did not feel he was necessary. "When the creative director asked him to stay, we all figured our new leader was a tyrant. The meeting continued for another hour or so. Finally, the new creative director sent us away with assignments—all of us in the room were to return the next day with our best idea for the campaign."

Josie continued to talk about how Mike was unmistakably bothered by the task. He quickly raised his hand and said, "I am not a creative guy." The creative director quickly replied, "But I think you are. In fact, I believe that you will come back with the best idea."

The following day, the team gathered in the conference room to share their concepts. "Mike looked disheveled," said Josie. "He looked beat up. He honestly looked scared."

One by one, each team member shared their ideas how we could win the jet company business. They had created posters and brochure ideas. They had created taglines, storyboards, and internet strategies. And Mike sat through it all silently.

The creative director, after we had all finished, turned toward Mike. "What'd you come up with?" he asked.

Mike stood. He wiped his sweaty forehead with his sleeve. In front of him was a small booklet that simply had pencil drawings on it. "I stayed up all night," said Mike. "You all know I am not very creative. So, the only thing I could think of was a campaign based around a passport—something we could mail, something we could turn into an app, and something that would engage all the potential and existing customers by helping them organize their itineraries but also give them information about the jet company."

The room was silent. The creative director stood, walked toward Mike, picked up the small pencil-drawn booklet and said, "Mike, I hate to say this, but this is horrible."

Mike responded sharply, "I told you it would be bad."

"No, the idea is brilliant," said the creative director. "The horrible thing is that you do not understand just how creative you are. This is outstanding."

"Every member of the creative team was smiling," said Josie. "We were all rooting for Mike. It was awesome." In fact, Josie told us that another designer leaned over to Mike and said, "Dude, I told you this was a fantastic idea. It's brilliant."

WHAT DO WE MEAN BY ENCOURAGE EFFORT?

Encouraging effort means promoting actions and ideas that lead to progress. It means recognizing the small things that matter. Sometimes it means urging a team member to test their boundaries, and sometimes it means removing the barriers for them, because they show a genuine passion in an area of the company, expertise, or an idea. Also, just as important, it means encouraging all team members to do the same—just like Mike's coworker had encouraged him. It is possible the encouragement from the team member to run with the idea was the one thing that made Mike not give up.

Typically, when we discuss encouraging effort with groups of leaders, we begin to see heads nod, as if everyone in the audience could tell us a story. And often they do tell us their stories. We met an outdoor sporting goods retail store manager who told us about a cashier he had hired. "We hired her because she had worked as a grocery store cashier. She had the technical capability to do the job but that's all we really expected. However, very quickly she started teaching us about different brands that we carried in the store. She knew the best hiking boots for wet terrain. She could easily share the benefits and weaknesses of different ski parkas. It turns out she was researching all of our products because she was passionate about understanding the differences between the products we carried—because she was a consumer of our products. Of course, we eventually moved her to the sales floor where she could share this knowledge with customers and other employees. However, we also wanted to encourage her passion for learning more, so we asked if she would take an active role training other employees. She loved it. Today, she is one of our best salespeople and leaders."

We also recently met a call center manager who has a stand-up meeting every day with her team and believes that it is the constant peer-to-peer encouragement that truly inspires effort. "I think a large portion of my role as a manager is to ensure that new employees or people who might need some encouragement are working closely with other employees known for cheering on their team members."

One of the biggest global peer-to-peer research studies ever conducted focused on how appreciation impacts engagement and shows that:[1]

- 30% of employees who said they "never/rarely" give recognition are engaged.

- 46% of employees who said they "sometimes" give recognition are engaged.

- 66% of employees who said they "often" give recognition are engaged.

- 81% of employees who said they "always" give recognition are engaged.

Think about this for a second. Overall, that is a 170% increase in the percentage of engaged employees when comparing employees who "never/rarely" give recognition to those that "always" give recognition. Of course, while there are definitely more aspects associated with engagement, having employees give recognition and notice the effort of their peers is clearly a great place to focus when trying to increase your team's engagement.

WHY EFFORT NEEDS ENCOURAGEMENT

Think about times when you were unsure if you were on track or in good standing and questioned your relationship with your leader. It is not a great feeling. Most likely you were less focused on doing the work and more distracted by self-talk such as, "Is what I am doing important or even noticed? Am I doing something wrong?" The focus shifts from the importance of your work to you and your value or lack thereof. Your confidence wanes, your work suffers, and distractions become more frequent and intense.

On the other hand, when you are not worried or distracted— because you are receiving praise—you focus on the work. That is why frequency is so important. It is not because we all need our egos stroked, but because it clearly communicates we are on track.

In fact, research clearly shows why encouraging effort fuels results.[2]

> **Employees reported:**
>
> - **An increased confidence in their skills.** They feel like they are good at their jobs and therefore expect more of their work, which increases their effort to do great work.
>
> - **They know they are on track and in good standing with their manager.** They do not question whether their leader is judging their work, and therefore don't spend their time worrying, but instead, spend it working.
>
> - **An improved relationship with their leader.** It is hard to like someone you may think doesn't like you or your work. Encouraging effort helps create a relationship between people that is based on positive communication, rather than waiting to communicate until a correction may be necessary.

Those responses in the research are hard to dismiss. However, the stories we have heard are impossible to dismiss, and, sadly, most of us have a negative story when it comes to receiving recognition for our efforts. We went the extra mile. We thought we were creating a difference people would love. And still, despite all the extra effort, no one noticed.

"I spent two weeks working nearly fourteen hours a day—long after everyone else had left the office—and no one noticed," wrote Brittney from North Carolina.

"My work helped win a huge client for the company. We had a group celebration, but no one said thank you to me for all that work and personal sacrifice."

Sebastian from London lamented, "I tried to impress my leaders for three beastly years. After a while I stopped trying. They did not care."

The pain of someone not recognizing your effort is not limited to the office. Melissa from Montreal shared, "I am a stay-at-home mother and part-time at-home worker. I appreciate the fact that my husband works hard. He is very appreciative of me and the way I have chosen to be home for our two children. My co-workers, however, even though they send me projects all day and night, don't seem to acknowledge the fact that I am working well beyond my parameters of being part-time—often staying up until 2:00 a.m. and rising early to meet deadlines. Ever since I decided to move to part time, I feel like no one notices my efforts—especially my team. I do not feel appreciated anymore."

As a final example, we chose to share Cory's personal experience.

"You have gotta make a change," said Cory's doctor. "Your diet needs to change. You need to start exercising."

These were words Cory expected. He knew he was overweight. He knew, at 49 years old, that his lifestyle was catching up to him. "I knew I had to put forth the effort," he said. "So, I did. I really did. I told my coworkers about my new diet. I told my friends that I was waking up early to walk. I asked my friends to work out with me. I challenged myself."

"I lost fifteen pounds within the first three weeks," he added. "I was proud. I was pushing myself every single day. I had a goal to lose sixty pounds total. And I know this sounds ridiculous, but I quit! Why? Because nobody noticed. It is embarrassing to say this because I know this is my situation to deal with, but I wished someone would've encouraged me."

None of us like to admit we need encouragement. We do not like the idea we cannot encourage ourselves to achieve great things. However, the truth is when we do give the effort—when we give it all we have got—and no one notices, it becomes extremely challenging to give that effort again, at work or anywhere else, for that matter.

For Cory, no one noticed. One simple comment would have encouraged him to keep going, try more, and stay committed. But it did not happen. Moreover, this story is all too common at work—people start to apply extra effort, it goes unnoticed, and they stop trying.

WHAT EFFORTS SHOULD YOU ENCOURAGE?

The expression on his face was either anger, frustration, or doubt. "I like what you guys are saying, and I think there are places for all this appreciation stuff," he said. "But, c'mon, am I really supposed to walk through the office each day telling everyone that they are doing a good job? Does everyone need a pat on the back each day?"

These words came from the franchise owner of numerous retail tire stores in the southwest region of the U.S. "I do not see all my guys on a daily basis. I cannot just show up and say 'good job.' How do I know who's giving extra effort? What am I looking for?"

In this franchise owner's particular case, it is challenging for him to know who's applying effort that deserves to be praised. However, he can ensure store managers are trained on what they should recognize each day. They should know when to praise effort. Maybe they notice an employee going out of his way to satisfy a demanding customer. Maybe they witness a team member motivating others. Or, possibly, they notice a certain employee's attention to organization ensures the shop is clean and well-ordered for the crew who comes in the morning.

In a less obvious example, Liz, who manages a tax accounting firm, explained, "All of our clients have different needs. The complexity of one person's taxes can differ greatly from another's. But the expectation of the outcome is always the same—accuracy. On a daily basis, it is hard for me to know who's giving extra effort. Sure, eventually we will know, but not on a day-to-day basis. When it comes to effort directed at great work, what should I be looking for? What should I be praising and recognizing?"

That is a common question we have been asked throughout the years, especially within an organization where employees' heads might be buried in their computer screen all day: "What efforts should I be looking to recognize?"

Overall, our research indicates it is important to recognize the effort that is directed toward the team's goals and purpose—the efforts an employee makes that are intended to create positive results.

Nevertheless, it is important to note that an employee's effort may not seem to be directly pointed at team goals. Instead, their efforts enable someone else in the organization to focus more specifically on those goals. For example, an executive assistant who books travel plans for his manager might see that her flight does not land until 11:45 p.m. He knows his manager well enough to know she probably didn't eat dinner, and, due to her dietary restrictions, he is concerned the central kitchen at the hotel will be closed by the time she checks in. So he calls ahead to have an appropriate meal delivered to his manger's room at her estimated time of arrival.

Obviously, feeding the manager is not directly related to the organizational goals of the company. Nevertheless, the effort and forethought of the executive assistant is valuable and deserves praise.

To understand which efforts deserve recognition, ask yourself the following questions:

- How will this effort, if continued, lead to a result that others value?

- Was the effort aligned with the team's goals?

- Was the effort intended to create a difference someone loved?

- Did the effort indirectly help someone else in their efforts to achieve a goal?

From the *New York Times* best selling book, *Great Work*: *How to Make a Difference People Love*, analysis of more than 10,000 detailed cases of award-winning work identified five key behaviors (things people do, rather than who people are) that lead to increased results.[3]

Encourage asking the right questions. When Marty Cooper was assigned to develop the first car phone, he paused and asked, "Why are we calling places—homes, offices, and cars—instead of calling people?" His question led to the invention of the mobile phone. When Denise, the Safety and Environmental Affairs Manager at Subaru's manufacturing plant in Lafayette, Indiana, a facility which produces approximately 180,000 vehicles per year, was tasked with reducing fifteen tons of landfill waste generated on a daily basis she asked, "Why not eliminate all waste?" Today, the plant is zero-landfill. Yes, that means you, as an individual, create more landfill waste each week than that entire plant. The point is these workers pause at the beginning of a project to think about the people or purpose their work serves. They consider customers, team members, leaders, and partners. They ask if they can make something easier, simpler, faster, safer, greener, or smarter. They ask if they can make it more affordable, convenient, enjoyable, connected, or secure. These "right" questions should be encouraged.

Encourage going and seeing. Employees should be encouraged to see how their work is being received. Just as the chef at a top restaurant might pop out of the kitchen to see the expressions on diners' faces as his beautiful entrées are placed before them, people who consistently perform award-winning work want to see how their work is being received. They get to find out firsthand what's working and what isn't. By seeing for themselves, they can find new ways of doing things that help the recipients of their work. We found that people who go and see their work being received are seventeen times more likely to have a passion for their work—because they have seen it being received.

Encourage new conversations. Instead of just initiating conversations with people in their work group, department, or close peers, leaders should encourage their team members to reach out to their "outer circle"—people who do not work within their department, company, or even industry. This way, employees can gather different points of view. A whopping 72% of people who produce award-winning work talk to their outer circle to get new perspectives, opinions, and ideas.

Encourage improving the mix. Small tweaks can produce massive results. Imagine the day someone decided to attach an eraser to the top of a pencil. It is a small change with a huge outcome. Leaders should encourage employees to see every project like this. They should encourage employees to look for ways to remove hurdles and make processes more efficient, improvements to add or subtract from a product, or ways they can give a customer a better experience. According to our research, work is three times more likely to be called important when someone has added or subtracted an element or two from a project, product, or process.

Encourage seeing it through. One of the most important things employees can do to produce their best work is to see the work all the way through until it makes a difference—and this often requires continuing encouragement. Too often, people think their work is done when it leaves their hands. In our research, we found that 90% of award-winning work projects include employees who remain involved through implementation and beyond.

Noticing these five actions, or any effort for that matter, can be difficult for many of us because we are all overwhelmed with our schedules and tasks that need to be accomplished. In today's world where telecommuting, remote, part-time or contract-based work are becoming more of the norm, noticing effort can be even more challenging. Just know, someone, somewhere, is doing something extra and would benefit by having their efforts noticed and praised.

HOW DO YOU TRAIN YOURSELF TO NOTICE EFFORT?

Get out of your office. If you are buried in your work area all day (or behind your computer screen, wherever you work), it is nearly impossible to see the efforts people are making. As a leader, it is your job to notice the effort and recognize the person. Get out of your office and go see people at work, whether that means in your building or out in the field where remote workers might be. Pay particular attention to those who are making good things happen, working extra (inside the office or at home), motivating others, getting noticed for their unique approaches, and are intent on making a difference.

Nolan Bushnell, the founder of Atari, detailed a recruiting practice he used to see how a potential applicant would not only think through a problem but also apply effort to a problem. Bushnell liked to hold hiring interviews at restaurants. He would ask the applicant how many pieces of gum they thought were underneath the tables. While some candidates would take a wild guess or say, "I have no idea," others would systematically count the tables, consider how long the restaurant was in business, and, based on the cleanliness of the space, hypothesize how often the bottoms of the tables were scraped. Of course, this situation was forced to see how much effort a candidate would put forth. But, by all accounts, it worked. Steve Jobs and Steve Wozniak, both employees of Atari at one time, were known to sleep under their desks because they did not want to leave until they solved a problem.

As leaders, it is our job to get out of our own world and into the unique worlds and personalities of others to encourage the efforts of those who work with us and for us.

Be curious. Simple questions like "How are you doing on the project?" or "What are you working on, and is there anything I can help you with?" can reveal a lot about how much effort people are giving toward achieving a difference-making outcome. Appreciate the people who are striving to find the right answer, struggling to overcome a hurdle, or even wrestling with frustration because they have not found the answer yet.

Listen. People applying extra effort will share ideas about how they could potentially solve a problem. They will ponder new approaches even if they do not voice their thoughts in their entirety. Listen carefully to the words and ideas that may be hidden beneath the blanket of "I just want you to think I am doing a good job." Moreover, when you hear an idea poking its head through their words, ask for a description and encourage, "Tell me what you are thinking about this. It sounds like you might be on to something." Then listen even more carefully.

Practice will make perfect as you apply these tips. In fact, as you read these suggestions you were probably reminded of efforts your employees are making that you have already noticed. That is great. However, unless you encourage those efforts, there is a good chance your team will stop applying those efforts.

HOW DO YOU ENCOURAGE EFFORT?

As we mentioned earlier, most managers were promoted because they were a star producer of individual results. You probably delivered results without much guidance. You just did it. You are not accustomed to asking for help or to things not working out. You may not be accustomed to struggling. But even if you have the ability to notice effort, you may not know how to properly encourage it. Start with these ideas.

Encourage people to test their boundaries. Most employees, when they accept a job or are assigned to a particular project, are given a task list or an explanation of expectations. Most of us are hardwired for the same thing—to meet expectations. Realize that people want to do great things. They want to be better. They want to be admired for their work. Unfortunately, many people often don't believe they can or should test their boundaries unless they are encouraged to flex, tackle a new project, and expand their current skill set. They do not think they have your permission. Encourage people in ways that will make it clear you support their efforts to test boundaries.

Words that encourage effort:

- "If anyone can pull this off, it's you."

- "I've got your back, and I think you can do it."

- "I think there's something special about the way you think that will help you nail this project."

Encourage people by removing hurdles. Become a bulldozer of obstacles that may be standing in people's way. Look to remove physical, emotional, process, and organizational limitations so people have the space to apply their intended effort.

Be an encouraging leader by giving:

- Approval of discretionary time to experiment and apply extra effort.

- Resources, whether it be financing, tools or equipment, or access to education or experts.

- Flexibility to explore within processes, departments, and titles or positions, even if the effort would not typically fall into their job description.

- Confidence and the permission to try and fail and keep trying. Give people the emotional support they need by allowing them to apply even more effort without the threat of being reprimanded if their effort does not at first achieve the intended goal.

Be warned: There is a huge difference between encouraging effort and demanding effort. Encouraging effort toward the achievement of great work means you are supporting people. Demanding effort, to the employee, often feels like their needs and goals are not being considered. Just like the Death Valley example we mentioned earlier, it is important to remember you cannot tell a flower when to bloom. You can only provide the conditions that enable it. Let's also not forget that engagement is an employee's choice—the decision to give extra effort and the willingness to go beyond the expected. At first, this may appear to be out of your control. You might think, "If an employee wants to give more, they will make that decision for themselves." However, we have found that unless you clearly communicate that you want people to test their boundaries and give their best effort, they do not always know they can or should.

Virgin Train headquarters in London, wanted to encourage specific efforts throughout their company—unique things the company valued that supported the brand to consumers and helped employees make this part of their culture. Most of us have probably seen these types of guides, whether they are in booklet form, within a handbook, or written on posters in corporate lunchrooms. However, Virgin Trains took a different approach. Instead of mild, forgettable platitudes that everyone else uses, consider the raw power of their words: "Screw Average. Create Amazing."

You really can't be any more specific and direct than "Screw Average." It's attention grabbing. It is explicitly telling employees they work for an organization that has a purpose and that employee attitudes and activities should be focused on fulfilling that purpose.

Of course, the phrases "Screw Average" and "Create Amazing" could be a powerful mantra all on their own. However, Virgin Trains wanted to ensure all employees had an idea of what those words looked like when they were turned into actions.

Shaking things up	**Innovation**
Giving a damn	**Boldness**
Fun	**Wow factor**

Again, those alone are interesting, attention grabbing, and fun concepts to think about when you consider they are all efforts encouraged by the company. However, it still wasn't enough for Virgin Trains, a company with a global reputation for being unique. The company took the time to explain each of the above. Although we will not share all the details here, we do want to illustrate how Virgin Trains explained the efforts they encourage by giving you the top two:

Shaking things up:	Giving a damn:
Quirky, spontaneous, different	Empowered and responsive people, working together
Free thinking and individual	Intuitive and flexible
Extraordinary, never mediocre	People not (just) protocol
Adrenaline	Doing the absolute best for people, doing the right thing

For Virgin Trains, these explanations clearly define the efforts they want to see from employees, and they communicate the efforts leaders should be encouraging.[4]

In your organization or team, what would the expectations be if they were clearly defined as just described? What are the efforts employees should be making, encouraging in each other, and being encouraged to make by leaders?

Being clear and concise, and communicating the efforts you want to encourage and want to see encouraged amongst peers creates a framework for people to follow. They know where to apply extra effort. They know what you value as their leader. And they also, through encouragement, help align each other toward a common goal.

CONNECT WORK TO A LARGER PURPOSE

Leaders are often required to communicate directives across different levels of the organization—from the top of the organization to middle management and all the way to the front line. And, as you probably already know, directives can sometimes just appear to be a simple task list of things that need to be done, without communicating why the tasks need to be done. That is why it is important to connect the tasks to the larger goals for your team. "Wash the windows" becomes "A Zagat reviewer will be in tonight or sometime this week. We want to get a five-star rating, so even the windows need to be spotless."

As a leader, you are probably also aware of the larger goals that aren't communicated company wide. For example, you may know of a large project happening in another department, and this awareness can create opportunities to encourage effort. "The IT department is under a ton of stress this week as they are moving servers. Although we in Accounting do not have a clue how to do their jobs, if you think of any way we can help, or even brighten their day, I'd love to hear your ideas."

Rory, a manager at a steel fabrication facility in Alberta, was recognized for encouraging his team to leave their workspace spotless after he overheard a salesperson mention he was giving a tour of the plant to a potential client later that evening. Rory told his team about the tour and asked if anyone had unique ideas to make their workspace impressive to the prospect. "There's only so much we can do," Rory explained, "but my team did the best they could to make our workspace clean and inviting. They also created a billboard that we hung on the back wall to welcome the client. All twelve of us signed the billboard."

As you can guess, the salesperson for the facility was tickled by the effort. And, even though the visitors did not become a client, the act of communicating to the entire staff when a new prospect is coming into the building has now become a standard procedure. In fact, it has become a competition among departments to see who can leave the most memorable welcoming gesture. These types of opportunities to encourage effort connect employees and their work to other outcomes and other people within the organization.

HOW MUCH ENCOURAGEMENT DOES EFFORT DESERVE?

Encouraging effort can be as simple as a pat on the back, a kind word of thanks, a handwritten note, or a small token of your appreciation. How you appreciate people depends on the level of effort you witness.

"My manager, Anton, heard me on the phone with a customer," said Julie, a loan officer at a bank in Minnesota. "I had only been working at the company for a couple of months. I had not seen any public displays of people being recognized, but when I hung up the phone, he started clapping. He asked everyone to stop what they were doing and explained, to the entire office, how I calmed a frustrated customer. I just thought I was being professional, you know? And it felt good, even though I was kind of embarrassed at first, to see that he was paying attention. Later that day I received a hand-written thank-you card from my manager stating, 'The bank values great service. I was proud to have you on the team, and honestly, I do not know if I would have handled the situation as well as you did.' Included in the card was a gift card to a local restaurant."

Julie's example reveals just one way to praise effort. Her manager decided to interrupt the team on the spot and show his appreciation. Of course, that is not the only way to praise effort. He could have waited until the end of the day to recognize her. He could have even waited until the morning meeting the next day to tell the entire team how well she handled the call. Or he could have just written the thank-you note to her. Praise can appear in many forms and formats depending on the personalities of the person giving the effort and the person praising the effort. The important thing is that it happens and in a timely fashion.

For larger efforts worthy of praise, you might consider public acknowledgment and gratitude (including a social media shout-out), a card or email, a gift card, or a small award. We heard of a ballet barre fitness studio whose owners thank their employees with Lulu Lemon headbands. It is not a lot monetarily, but it makes a huge impact, especially when the presentations are made public. Other more progressive companies give points in a company-wide recognition program. Our own client studies show when presentations are public, employees are 10–30% more likely to recommend the company as a great place to work, they're more likely to feel as if they fit in and belong, and they feel the company cares about them.[5]

Some people aren't sure exactly what they should say. Others question when is the best timing. And it can be challenging to know exactly how much to spend. After years of worldwide research, we think we have a pretty good idea of what works best, how often it should happen, the impact it makes, and the feelings it creates.

WHAT NOT TO DO WHEN ENCOURAGING EFFORT

Jose was offended by how his manager said thank you—he asked Jose to walk him to his car as he shared his appreciation, because "He said he had something important to attend to." Svetta's leader called her to discuss something entirely different, and when the conversation was wrapping up, he said, almost threateningly, "By the way, everything you are doing to make this deadline is appreciated."

While both of these examples might feel better than nothing, they actually are not. People receiving appreciation feel like their efforts are taking a back seat to something more pressing, and that can do more harm than good. You could possibly compare it to calling your spouse on your anniversary to tell them how much you love them but won't be able to go to dinner tonight because some colleagues are headed out for happy hour.

Here are a few guidelines to follow when encouraging effort and showing appreciation in person or over the phone.

Make it face-to-face, if possible. If you walk to the employee's office or desk to show appreciation, make it your primary task. Of course, we all get busy during the day and often need to multi-task. Nevertheless, we do not want to dilute what could be a powerful and impactful conversation by making appreciation just another item on our checklist. Make it clear that you are coming to speak to them individually, and that is why you left your office or desk—to show your appreciation to them. If you are not in the same geographic location, use technology like Skype or FaceTime so they can see you. If meeting face- to-face just is not possible, make a phone call.

Make recognition the only reason for the call. If you must express your appreciation over the phone, make it the only reason for your call. Ask them, "Did I catch you at a good time to talk?" And don't bring up a bunch of other items on the to-do list at the end of the call. Save those items for another conversation.

Make it timely. Do you remember three and half months ago when you insisted the last sentence of that document be checked for mistakes one last time before being sent to a client? Do you remember sitting at your house that night and working over every detail, over and over, until you were sure it was perfect? Do you remember going to your team the next day and telling them how much time you spent? No. You do not remember that. The reason you do not remember it is because no one seemed to care. You did not get a thank you. You did not get a pat on the back. And if someone came to you today and said, "Your extra effort three months ago deserves to be praised," you would almost feel offended.

Effort is applied on a daily, weekly, monthly, and even yearly basis. However, none of us want to get praised for our effort months later.

Research by the O.C. Tanner Institute shows that for small efforts, such as when a person helps out a team member, praise needs to happen daily. For example, you help a stressed colleague finish a project by gathering input and taking notes in a meeting they were supposed to attend. You hope they thank you for that help the same day, or, if nothing else, the next day. Alternatively, let's say an employee on your team shows up early to organize the meeting room and outline the entire agenda on a whiteboard to save time, even though they were not asked to do so. A thank you delivered later that day, or an e-card expressing your gratitude would be appropriate praise.

WHAT IF YOU ENCOURAGE EFFORT AND THEIR ATTEMPT FAILS?

"I have always told my employees, 'If you do not fail within your first year of employment, I will fire you,'" Jay Samit revealed during an interview.[6] Samit is widely recognized as one of the world's leading experts on disruption and innovation. He has helped grow pre-IPO companies such as LinkedIn and eBay, held senior management roles at Sony and Universal Studios, and pioneered breakthrough advancements in mobile video, Internet advertising, e-commerce, social networks, eBooks, and digital music that are used by billions of consumers.

"I have failed more than anyone I know," Samit claimed. "If people are not failing, then they are not really trying to improve something. You can't find true success without failing."

Those might seem like rogue words from a guy who has built a reputation based on being a disruptive innovator. But we agree with him. If an effort is pointed toward creating progress—and failure would not produce dismal outcomes for the organization—then effort must be actively encouraged, noticed, praised, and even rewarded. Remember, employees enter organizations with the belief they can make a difference. If their intentions are good, their effort to produce great work must be encouraged.

HOW TO WRITE AN EFFECTIVE THANK-YOU NOTE

Whether writing a hand-written note or an email:

Include the date. Although it might seem unnecessary, a dated note shows the recipient the exact day you were thinking about them and appreciating their effort. They might see it and think, "Oh, that was Thursday. I didn't even see or talk to her on Thursday. It's nice she was thinking of me."

Write a salutation with their name. Researchers in the direct marketing world have stated that the most powerful word in the English language is: "you." Apparently, we like the idea that a sentence, offer, or question is specifically addressed to us. Nevertheless, the word "you" doesn't hold a candle to seeing your own name. It sends a message that the writer is being personal, appreciating our work in particular.

Specifically address the great work you saw, heard about, or experienced. Generic thank you messages don't create a big impact. But if the recipient of a note sees that you know specifically what they are working on, what they did, and who they did it for, they'll truly feel appreciated.

Express why a person's actions or efforts mean something.
People need to understand that the difference they made was loved.
Express in your note who the recipient of their work was, why it
benefited them or the organization, and how it aligns with the values
of your company. Unless people are directly told why their efforts
matter to a bigger purpose, they won't necessarily know how their
work belongs in the bigger picture, and they might not repeat the
behavior. Expressing why a person's specific actions or efforts mean
something special shows them the path for their future efforts.

November 20, 2017

Dear Jacob,

I wanted to let you know how much I appreciate your extra
effort over the past couple of months. I know you've been
working hard and working extra hours. The ideas you have
about improving workflow processes are big and bold. You were
the only person to question our current (and admittedly
outdated) processes. This type of thinking is highly valued in
this company. We take great pride in leading the industry.
It's people like you who make that happen.

Thank you. You have displayed an exemplary definition of what
great work truly means. Keep it up. Continue challenging the
process to make it better!

With Appreciation,
Katherine

QUICK TAKE

Encouraging Effort Makes a Difference:
- Employees experience increased confidence in their skills.
- Employees know they are on track and in good standing.
- Employees have an improved relationship with their leader.

Encouraging Effort Can Be Accomplished By:
- Shout-out in team meeting.
- Handwritten note, email, eCard, or social network praise.
- Gift cards or points in a recognition program.

Frequency:
- Extra Effort should be encouraged daily and weekly.

Keep In Mind:
- Make it timely.
- Make it in person, if possible.
- Make it the only reason for the conversation.

Be Supportive:
- Encourage team members to test the boundaries.
- Plan time and space for team members to apply their effort.
- Provide resources (financing, tools or equipment, access to education or experts).
- Give permission to try and fail and keep trying.

If you want to keep yourself on task and stay organized so you can encourage effort more often, subscribe to the O.C. Tanner company's free monthly appreciation calendar or appreciation tip emails at www.octanner.com/subscribe.

CHAPTER 6

REWARD RESULTS

Better-than-expected results don't just happen. They are always the culmination of extra effort, ingenuity, collaboration, caring, and gritty persistence. The journey to great results is hampered by obstacles, limitations, lack of resources, and the ever-present gravitational forces that protect the status quo. After interviewing hundreds of people who delivered extraordinary results, it was obvious that outstanding results only came to fruition because people chose to do more than they were paid to do. Annette, whose work on a multi-month process-improvement project resulted in saving her company over $3 million, said it this way, "The whole point of great work, is to put your heart and soul into something. Not because you were told to, but because you want to do something that makes a difference." Work that delivers that kind of difference is to be respected, prized, celebrated, and rewarded.

Great work—whether it be the creation of a better strategy, the pursuit of new thinking, the back-breaking work of manual labor, the long hours invested in improving something, or the ideas that change the world around us—leads to improved results. Some are small. Some contribute in more noticeable ways. Others lead to significant outcomes. Behind each result is always an interesting story. Consider the following example from a world-class media company.

"Lisa delights in tackling even the most challenging problems and is always brainstorming ways to make things bigger, better, and faster," said Lisa's manager. "Her energy is infectious and she makes those around her stronger, more creative, and helps them think outside the box. She has the uncanny ability to spot a weakness, methodically and critically prioritize varied solutions, and effectively collaborate with others to implement the chosen solution. More importantly, she takes it one step further by doing the most challenging aspect of all, which is documenting the process end to end."

Unarguably, those beautifully summarized words alone are enough to send an employee's attitude soaring with pride. They can inspire others to emulate Lisa's attitude toward work. However, the irony is that these words only convey Lisa's efforts. And the results she created are much more impressive.

"When Lisa was hired fourteen months ago, we hoped that she could help wade through the countless 'How-To' documents. We never imagined that she would completely restructure them and, in turn, drastically improve the entire day-to-day functions of our group."

This media company, although one of the biggest in the world, was struggling, as many companies do, with outdated, or in the words of the manager, "archaic," processes of distributing necessary information both internally and externally.

"Lisa saw our excessive reliance on time-consuming monitoring and tracking of clients and products, and quickly researched ways to modernize it. Her willingness to look beyond the tools in front of her and not be paralyzed by the unknown, but instead be challenged by it, has redefined how we function as a team."

Obviously, results are measured in all sorts of ways. In some organizations, results may be measured in bottom line numbers. In others, in may be time spent, waste eliminated, patients treated, people educated, or injuries decreased. For different jobs, results can mean increasing customer satisfaction, team output, decreases in defective products, or the creation of new customer relationships. In fact, sometimes the biggest results can come from something very simple—a fresh perspective.

Robert, for example, works for a large global manufacturing company. He recognized an opportunity to sell an existing product in a new way—instead of selling through existing channels, they would target an entirely different kind of customer. "He consistently positioned a different package size and design to our marketing team and worked across packaging, regulatory, and label groups to write a new label for the packaging, including an updated product bar code for the customers' ease of inventory and sale," said Robert's manager. "These efforts have already secured a big new customer, which will result in an additional $1.3 million in sales. A creative selling idea, new packaging, and great teamwork with our marketing team led to a significant increase in sales and revenue, not to mention a curiosity within the organization to see which other products could be repositioned to sell to a new client base."

WHAT DO WE MEAN BY REWARD RESULTS?

Rewarding results means recognizing and rewarding people who have produced a measurable impact. Typically, when we talk about rewarding results, we are talking about rewarding a difference someone has made that is not just an expectation. For example, just getting work finished as part of an employee's job description is to be appreciated. However, taking a project to the next level is deserving of special recognition.

Consider the work of Petri, a web designer. She works for a software company that typically sells an off-the-shelf product. Most of her design focuses on internal needs. When she was approached by the head of sales asking if she could help create a presentation so the company could pitch a full-service product to a Fortune 100 company, including support, training, and consultation, Petri jumped at the chance. She designed a persuasive slide presentation. She created handouts that covered the details and functionality the software could offer the potential client, including descriptions of the support they would receive. And although the sales team was happy to show the functionality of the software during the presentation branded to the software company, Petri took her job to the next level. She approached the programming team to find out how hard it would be to integrate the potential client's logo and brand into a few functional pieces of the software so the potential client could see and feel what the software looked like integrated with their current branding. "We got the contract because the client said we were the only company who took the time to incorporate their brand and offer full support and training," said Petri's manager. "It was a huge win for the company."

Rewarding results is critical. Significant achievements—like Annette, Lisa, Robert, and Petri's—that support the company's values and business goals—whether the person achieves a sales goal, implements an innovative idea, improves a process or provides exceptional customer service—is worthy of more than a thank you.

Imagine how undervalued all of these people would have felt if they knew they went above and beyond what was asked of them, and all they received was a pat on the back.

Rewarding results is different from encouraging effort in that the reward comes after, rather than before, the result is realized. Achievements obviously come at different levels, with differing results, for the team or organization, and should be rewarded accordingly.

They should be rewarded with something that:

- Shows the value of the accomplishment.

- Is symbolic of the work that was done to achieve the goal.

- Recognizes the work in front of team members so other members of the team can celebrate the victory and understand what the organization values.

RECOGNITION AWARDS ARE NOT INCENTIVES

In the examples we provided earlier, it is important to realize each of them were not incentivized by receiving a reward for their work. Take Petri for example, she went above and beyond because she wanted to make a positive difference to win the new customer. There is a big difference between incentives and rewards. Incentives are presented as something predefined that is earned by an employee. It is a quid-pro-quo transaction built on the premise that, "If you do A, then you get B." Recognition awards, on the other hand, are given as meaningful symbols of appreciation for a job well done—not as a pre-agreed response to the attainment of a goal.

Incentives are valuable in certain job functions and situations, but should not be confused with recognition. Mixing them up and treating them as the same thing is a dangerous practice due to employees' perceptions of the situation and the different emotions that accompany each. Because incentives are earned, they require specific rule structures, accurate measurement, and clearly communicated criteria. Consider the difference between these two situations.

Situation 1: If a manager at a grocery store asks an employee to sweep the floor, and the employee sweeps the floor, the results (while they may be praiseworthy) are not deserving of a reward. If the manager offers a reward for keeping the floors swept perfectly every day, and that employee achieves the goal, the employee is being incentivized.

Situation 2: Let's say one of the grocery store's values is to provide every customer with a safe, clean, and healthy experience. The employee who was tasked with sweeping the floors wants to ensure company values are being upheld—and wants all employees to be concerned about the cleanliness of the floors. The employee has an idea. He creates a competition between the day and night shifts. With approval from both the day and night managers, the employees begin to challenge their coworkers and work as a team and consistently look for small pieces of trash that can be discarded or any dirt or debris that can be cleaned throughout the shift. They challenge the managers to make surprise visits during the opposing team's shift and look for things that could be cleaned. Each piece of trash or debris found counts against the shift team. The team with the fewest infractions wins. This, obviously, is an incentive for the teams. However, the employee—the one who created a new, fun, results-oriented plan—deserves to be recognized and receive a reward for the improved results. The employee needs to understand the result he created made a difference. A cleaner store throughout a shift is a small result, but it's a highly appreciated result that deserves to be rewarded. Small results deserve rewards just like big results, and the reward needs to reflect the value of the results created.

A recognition reward is a sincere gesture of appreciation for creating a result that was valued. The employee now has a sense of pride in what he accomplished, an emotional connection to the reward (a feeling his idea and work is appreciated) and the manager (for noticing the effort and the result achieved).

ISN'T "THANK YOU" ENOUGH?

One of the most common questions we hear from leaders and organizations is, "Do I really need to give them something? Isn't saying thank you enough?" The answer, in most circumstances, is no. As we mentioned, results come in all sizes, and so do rewards. Moreover, from small results and small rewards to large results and large rewards, research shows the impact of rewarding results far exceeds mere praise when it comes to inspiring people to create improved results. In fact, global research shows that for employees, rewarding results creates a focus on outcomes that drive improved results.

Rewarding results can:

- Encourage employees to seek new ways to improve efficiency.

- Increase efforts to ensure customers are happy.

- Increase willingness to put in a great deal of effort.

Remember, people want to do great work. They want their work to make a difference, and the ideas above are examples of influencers that show employees you appreciate the results they are creating—both big and small.

REWARD MYTHS AND REALITIES

Some leaders hesitate to give rewards for great work for a variety of mythical reasons. The most common objections we hear are:

Myth: People should not be rewarded for doing their job. These leaders will argue that they hired people to meet an expectation in exchange for a paycheck. We do not disagree. However, these leaders are overlooking one huge gap—the difference between expected results and extraordinary results. **Reality:** Employees who go above and beyond deserve more than a paycheck because they delivered much more value than was expected.

Myth: It will seem like they are playing favorites. These leaders are concerned that giving a reward to one person might make another person feel bad.

Reality: People who do great work should be rewarded more than those people who do good work. You don't pay everyone the same salary, why would you recognize them the same?

Myth: They will expect it every time. Some leaders worry it may become an entitlement.

Reality: People are happy to have their work appreciated. If this leads to more great work, the investment in recognizing that great work will fund itself.

WHICH RESULTS SHOULD BE REWARDED AND HOW?

Similar to encouraging effort, results that deserve to be rewarded are those that are most important to the team or organization's objectives. The results to be rewarded are not those that are expected. We have two categories of results: victories and highest achievements—all of which deserve a different level of reward and celebration, because the results come in various sizes. The award and the level of presentation needs to match the result.

REWARDING VICTORIES

A victory might be creating a successful new product. It might be landing a big client. Alternatively, it might be a new process that saves the team or company time and money. Victories, usually involve stick-with-it goals that take determination. With victories of all sizes, employees feel a heightened sense of value, an increased sense of pride, and an elevated sense of accomplishment within the organization. Victories should be celebrated.

For example, Victoria is Director of Safety, Health, and Wellness at a warehousing company. For many years she had focused on making the company accident-free, but over the past couple of years (because the company's safety program was so effective), she began digging into another issue—lack of participation in the company wellness program. Victoria conducted research on what other companies were doing to increase participation in their programs. She carried out internal surveys to find out why her company was getting such low participation. Moreover, she asked employees what they wanted for their health. After fourteen months, Victoria was proud to launch the company's improved wellness program. Participation skyrocketed the first year, increasing from 12% to 41%. Obviously, Victoria wants to increase participation even further in the future, but this was definitely a big win, and a victory for Victoria deserving of recognition and reward.

WHAT IS AN APPROPRIATE AWARD FOR A VICTORY?

The value of the award should reflect the value that was created by the employee or team. Tirelessly working to land a multimillion-dollar client deserves a bigger award than a gift card to the local coffee shop. We heard from an employee who drove many hours to meet with a client and convince them to continue their long-standing relationship with his company instead of switching to another vendor, as they had been planning. When his manager learned of his extraordinary efforts and its positive outcome, the manager nominated him for an award in their corporate reward program, which allowed the employee to choose the gourmet cookware he had always wanted, and which was meaningful to him as he loved to cook.

A tangible award becomes a lasting symbol of accomplishment. Whenever a contributor looks at or uses their award, it reminds them of their victory and the feelings they have about their team and company who appreciated their work.

HOW DO YOU CELEBRATE A VICTORY?

All victories should be recognized as close to the accomplishment as possible by you and your team. However, some victories can also be celebrated and shared with a larger group when the result is significant enough. Maybe the quick completion of an unexpected project could be recognized at weekly team meetings. But if that project turns into a revenue game-changer for the organization, it could also be recognized at a monthly or quarterly all-staff meeting.

With all victories, it's your responsibility as a leader to talk about what the employee did to achieve the results. Talk about why the results are valued by the team and organization. And, especially with bigger victories, share some of the details about the hurdles the employee had to overcome, the challenges they faced, and the tenacity that got them across the finish line for the big victory.

Little victories may happen weekly or monthly, and depending on the role of the employee, possibly even more often. They deserve to be recognized quickly, and the awards, appropriate to the results, show the employee that their work is valuable in producing the results they are achieving.

Medium-sized victories may happen a few times per year, often at the end of a project, the attainment of a goal, or at the conclusion of an improvement initiative or other specific accomplishment.

Big victories come less often but are incredibly important to celebrate. They are the wins that often define our careers. They are the things we recall in the years to come. They give us pride. They give us the energy to do it again. Moreover, they inspire those around us to create big victories for themselves.

HOW DOES REWARDING VICTORIES IMPACT AN EMPLOYEE?

Research shows recognizing victories:

- Inspires innovation, productivity, and performance.

- Creates feelings of appreciation and visibility that serve as a lasting reminder of the accomplishment.

- Boosts morale and increases pride within the company.

Consider this big victory appreciation moment and the impact it had on Sasha, who was shocked to receive the Inspiration of the Year Award at a specialty foods company in Australia—an award that is typically reserved for sales leaders.

"I had been out of the workforce for nearly ten years as I raised my children from home," she said. "I also had never been a salesperson before. In fact, my background was in public relations. So I knew I needed to work hard my first year back at work. I never dreamed that my second year back I would win this kind of award, because at the time I wasn't one of the top producers. However, when they presented me with this award, my colleagues began sharing stories about how my unconventional approach was inspiring them to try new things, push harder, and ultimately close more deals, which impacted the sales results of the company. I have always prided myself on being a tough girl but I cried like a baby at that banquet. I love this company, the people, and the opportunity. I no longer feel like the new kid."

HIGHEST ACHIEVEMENTS

Maybe a sales representative consistently lands the biggest clients and breaks an all-time company record. Maybe an engineer innovates an industry-wide game-changing product. Maybe a member of the legal department protects previously overlooked company assets which creates an entirely new revenue stream for the organization. Or maybe a seasoned department leader consistently delivers such outstanding results over an extended period of time that it warrants the highest form of recognition the company can give.

Highest achievements are reserved for extraordinary results. They are the accomplishments we achieve within a body of our work and generally only happen a few times within a career.

For example, Ira was working as a business development specialist at a nutritional supplements manufacturer. The company was known for making custom products for its clients—primarily naturopathic and chiropractic offices who wanted to offer their patients high quality supplements. Ira wondered if they were overlooking additional distribution possibilities for these custom supplement formulations and began approaching big-box retail stores with the idea of private labeling. After many months and a lot of ground work, when he came back to the office one day he announced he had arranged a meeting with the big-box retailer executives. His leader was thrilled. Ira's work resulted in a partnership that changed the company's financial trajectory overnight. Now the small supplement producer is selling more products to one retail client than all their other clients combined.

WHAT IS AN APPROPRIATE REWARD FOR A
HIGHEST ACHIEVEMENT?

When it comes to the highest honor and recognition an employee can receive, our research shows that symbolic awards are critical to the appreciation felt by the recipient—this is like the gold medal, the Oscar, the lifetime achievement award, the champion of awards. These awards are often called President's Awards, Founder's Awards, or other names that signal to everyone the importance of the accomplishment. Often the award itself is accompanied by a large cash award, or a generous gift or trip. The symbolic award is one that is cherished for life. It sits on display shelves, mantels, and inside glass cases as it signifies the ultimate performance and the ultimate appreciation.

The significance of a symbolic award and the value to the recipient far outweighs the monetary value of the award because of the emotional connection to the accomplishment. The award symbolizes the thinking, planning, hours involved (sometimes years involved), and the personal sacrifice involved in achieving the results. It symbolizes the respect earned, the talents portrayed, and the ultimate achievement.

HOW DO YOU CELEBRATE A HIGHEST ACHIEVEMENT?

Organizations handle highest achievements differently. More often than not the person being recognized is celebrated in front of a large group, like at a company event. Instead of just talking about the results achieved, the process of achieving is discussed—this could include small victories that led to the achievement, seemingly impossible odds that were overcome, or a complete shift in thinking that revolutionizes something huge. Again, the value of the work and the results are shared in detail. The story of hurdles and challenges throughout the project are shared along with appreciation from the entire audience, because the highest achievement impacted a major portion of, or even the entire, organization.

For the recipient of the award, this level of recognition is critical to their future with the organization. If overlooked or undermined, the employee will leave the organization and seek the appreciation (and generate the results) somewhere else. Of course, lack of appreciation and recognition will eventually cause employees to leave regardless of how big or small that employee's achievements are. However, with highest achievements, the lack of appreciation is amplified because highest achievements are obvious—to the person who achieved, and all those who witness the achievement. The ramifications of not recognizing a highest achievement are greater.

HOW DOES REWARDING HIGHEST ACHIEVEMENTS
IMPACT THE EMPLOYEE?

Research shows rewards for highest achievements create:

- Feelings of value.

- Alignment to highest levels of company goals.

- Pride in receiving the ultimate symbol of accomplishment.

In a conversation with a recent recipient of a highest achievement award, Derek described his experience: "About three weeks ago, I received the President's Award, which was awesome. They invited my wife and daughter to come, which meant a lot. The executive that I report up to was there and the CEO was as well. There was also a co-worker on the phone whom I had been working with for months to make sure all our processes were running smoothly through a big project. At the beginning of the presentation, my colleague on the phone spoke about why she had nominated me. I was in front of the whole executive team, standing there with my wife and my one-year-old child, and it felt amazing. Working both in the office and from home, being able to share that moment with my wife, having her see how well I am appreciated, it felt good. Moreover, that the sacrifices that she makes were also appreciated—I think she was able to connect that. I have received many awards in the past, but to have my wife hear the presentation was special. They also presented me with a special award, which was cool, because it is something tangible. Points are awesome. I can purchase a gift card for a hotel, so my wife and I can enjoy a weekend away or something. However, that award I get to have on my desk serves as a constant reminder that my work was appreciated. And that feels really good."

Derek's award presentation included all the best things recognition can deliver: a personalized expression of appreciation, a symbolically meaningful award, and a public presentation. However, to him, it stood out because his family also got to be a part of the presentation.

Appreciation, recognition, and rewards for victories small and significant, and highest achievements have a huge impact on employees. These rewards form powerful memories of the results created. And the awards become cherished items—holding a sentimental and emotional value far beyond the actual value of the award because they are reminders of effort, skill, intention, and commitment to achieving a goal. In fact, these awards have symbolic value, which, as research has shown us throughout the years, has an impact that is deeply meaningful.

THE POWER OF A SYMBOL

What do these awards mean to the person who receives them? While it is true that a job well done is a reward in itself and satisfaction is felt from achieving any goal, research shows that when results are achieved, appreciation is best communicated when a symbolic award is presented to the person who achieved the success. An award validates and affirms that an employee and their work are valued by their team, their leaders, and their organization.

If you've ever watched the Winter Olympics or the X Games, you may be familiar with Shaun White, who seems to soar through the air like he might never return to the ground. White, a professional snowboarder, is a two-time Olympic Gold Medalist and holds the record at the X Games for gold medals, as well as overall number of medals won.

What's interesting about Shaun is that whenever you see him in an interview, you can't help but notice the Olympic athlete rings on his fingers. There are four of them, all representing Olympic events he has competed in. All representing the work, the courage, and we're sure the wipe-outs, that have earned him celebrity status in the snowboarding world. All symbolic of the moments and achievements that make him who he is today. Consider the significance of winning a Nobel Prize, or an Oscar, or a Gold Record—or Shaun White's rings. All of these awards have a monetary value. But that monetary value pales in comparison to the sentimental value of the symbol. Just like these medals and rings and statues, rewards for results are perceived as more valuable than their monetary value because they are meaningful. In fact, lasting awards for results are more desirable than money itself. Our research shows that when employees are asked the following questions, rewards (along with purposeful recognition) far surpass a 5% bonus, which most leaders don't have the ability to give anyway.[1]

Which of the following increases your efforts to ensure customers are happy?

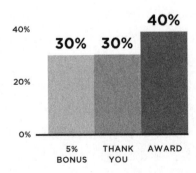

Which of the following is most impactful in encouraging you to proactively seek new ways of doing things?

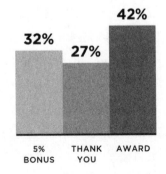

CREATING A PROCESS FOR REWARDING RESULTS

"I was surprised that she knew me," wrote Jacob, a software engineer in London. "My manager, Lillian, took the time to think about me. I grew up in Southern California riding a skateboard. I still like to skate and use a board for transportation when I can. After the completion of a big project, she asked me if skating around the city was the same as it was in California. Of course, I responded that it's not. London is much older than Huntington Beach. There's no strand or boardwalk. And I told her that although there are boards that handle the rough sidewalks better, I haven't been able to find one here. Admittedly, I hadn't looked very hard. But she did. She found me one. She thanked me for the work I had done on the project and handed me a longboard. It's still not easy to skate through London. But the thought was there. She wanted to give me something that I would love."

Highly personalized awards, like Jacob's longboard, are very thoughtful. Hearing stories about leaders who knew their employees and their hobbies and interests so well they could go out and find the perfect award is impressive. However, we know that many leaders find the process of choosing the appropriate award daunting. This is where a company-wide recognition program becomes extremely beneficial— offering a selection of awards that allows employees to choose items that are of particular value to them. Most corporate recognition programs also allow employees to accumulate reward points that they can exchange for awards that fit their lifestyle. By using points instead of cash values, the focus remains on the recognition instead of the monetary value of the award itself.

The critical factor, whether you choose to reward results with carefully thought-out skateboards and other items or choose to incorporate into a recognition program, is to not miss those critical moments to reward improved results.

I DON'T LIKE TO FEEL OBLIGATED

Many leaders reported being concerned when their organization introduced a recognition program. "I worried that they were turning something that should be sincere, genuine, and heartfelt into something procedural," Alex, a warehouse manager for a large retail store explained. "I loved the idea, but I didn't want it to become something that was a corporate obligation. It did feel a little procedural, at first. Until I did it and used the tools. That's when I saw sincerity flow like never before—from managers to employees and from employees to other employees. That's when you see changes in people—their efforts, their commitment, and their relationship toward the team."

The goal of a structured recognition program isn't to drown the sincerity and emotion that accompany true appreciation, but instead, it's to establish a strategy and process that inspires more sincerity and emotion. In fact, many forward-thinking companies use corporate-wide technology to support programs that will help build a culture where people cheer for each other so no victory goes unappreciated or unrewarded. Technology simply allows and promotes alignment with values and communicates the importance of accomplishments. Being strategic with recognition doesn't create an obligation for you. It creates an opportunity for you, because when your people do great work, the organization, your team, you as the leader, and that employee will reap the benefits.

Great organizations also use social tools and technologies to share moments of appreciation company-wide, to give visibility to everyone about the great work happening all over the company. Again, technology can be used to make what you want to do—appreciate—easier, more engaging, and more impactful. In fact, you'll become a better leader when you leverage tools available to you to integrate recognition into your day-to-day leadership practices.

WHAT NOT TO DO WHEN REWARDING RESULTS

Numerous studies have proven that purposeful employee recognition can fuel engagement, accelerate performance, and build strong workplace cultures. But can recognition go wrong? It can, and it does. We hear some of these stories from time to time. Here are the most common mistakes we've heard from employees all over the world.

The manager takes credit: It's absolutely cringe-worthy when a leader brings an employee in front of their team and takes credit for what they did by saying something like, "You've done a great job, and when I pointed you in the right direction, you succeeded."

Recognition is a mystery: A number of people in focus groups we've conducted reported receiving a mysterious package on their desk, in their mailbox, or on their chair. As much as people may like surprises, the mystery recognition gesture not only loses its meaning, but it also marginalizes any recognition the employee receives in the future. What is it for? Is this how they appreciate me?

Filling quotas: Yes, research has proven that frequent recognition increases employee performance. But simply filling a manager "recognition quota" is a dangerous practice. Picture a leader standing in front of her team and sincerely recognizing Marta for several months of hard work and ultimately her flawless execution of a finance system upgrade. The team applauds her. Then the leader says something that immediately marginalizes the sentiment. "Marta, thanks for doing what you did, we really appreciate it. And because Bill and Stephen haven't been recognized in a long time, I have a couple of awards for them as I'm sure they deserve some recognition too. So keep up the good work everyone." Bill and Stephen get the same recognition as Marta? For what? Did anyone win?

The timing is bad: One of the complaints employees have reported is that they receive a recognition presentation, but it's extremely late. A quote from one focus group member: "After working my butt off for nearly six months, completing my project early, and giving them more than they asked for, my manager didn't say anything until two months later when he took the team out for lunch. At that point, I thought he didn't even know if I had completed the project."

They don't know their audience: The examples we've heard of this deadly mistake can sound funny at first. But they're not. When a person who hates coffee gets gift cards to a coffee shop as a reward, or a remote worker receives a gift card to a store that doesn't exist in their country, the message being sent by the manager is not "I appreciate you" but instead it's, "I don't even know you." What if your employees took as little time to know the company as you did to know them?

It's all a song and dance: The number one complaint from focus groups around the world about recognition is that it wasn't sincere.

Nobody wants to receive an obligatory recognition gesture. They want to be appreciated. They want to feel their efforts are making an impact that people value. But if they feel they're being patronized, their effort, attitude, and commitment to a leader and a company will fizzle fast. Being fake with employees can seal any manager's fate.

Playing favorites: We understand that all companies are going to have star players who legitimately deserve consistent appreciation. But we've also heard a lot of employees complain about managers playing favorites with some employees who might be friends. Employees quickly pick up on the favoritism and lose respect for both the manager and the significance of the recognition.

It's a guilt thing: This is when a manager uses rewards to somehow apologize for their own bad or rude behavior. We talked to someone who said she knew who would get the next award in a team meeting based on who their manager had chewed out the previous week. The employees know when guilt is driving the reward and therefore deem any reward as a bit of an insult.

Simple mistakes in any recognition presentation are typically forgiven by employees because they still appreciate the intention—the sincerity behind the effort. However, it's easy to see in these eight "Not-To-Dos" how recognition done wrong could quickly be the death of a manager's positive influence.

WHAT TO SAY AT A RECOGNITION PRESENTATION

When it comes to rewarding results, what you say and how you say it really matters. To plan what you will say, think about someone who deserves your recognition. Here is a simple way to ensure you do it well. We use an acronym to keep it easy to remember—SAIL. Fill out this simple worksheet to help you craft a personal and meaningful presentation.

Person to be recognized: _____

Situation—What was the challenge or opportunity the person was faced with?

_____

_____

Action—What specific actions did the person take to overcome the challenges?

_____

_____

Impact—What difference did their actions make for the customer, team, or organization?

_____

_____

Link—How did their actions link to what the team or organization values?

_____

_____

Finally, think about how you can make this recognition experience personal:

_____

_____

_____

_____

_____

_____

_____

To download a copy of this form, go to www.octanner.com/appreciatebook.

QUICK TAKE

Rewarding results means recognizing and rewarding people who have produced a measurable impact on a product or process, inside a team or department, or on the entire organization. Typically, when we talk about rewarding results, we are talking about rewarding a difference someone has made that is not just an expectation. A recognition reward is not an incentive, but is a sincere gesture of appreciation for creating a result that was valued.

Rewarding Results Makes a Difference By:
- Inspiring innovation, productivity, and performance.
- Creating feelings of appreciation and visibility that serves as a lasting reminder of the accomplishment.
- Boosting morale and increasing pride with the company.

Small Victories Can Be Rewarded By:
- Points in a recognition program, gifts, or gift cards.
- Handwritten note, email, eCard, or social network praise.

Significant Victories Deserve More Significant Rewards That Can Include:
- Formal recognition in a team or department meeting.
- Symbolic award that serves as a reminder of achievement.
- Points in a recognition program, gifts, or gift cards.

Highest Achievements Should Be Rewarded By:
- Formal recognition in a division or company meeting.
- Symbolic award that serves as a reminder of achievement.
- Merchandise award and/or significant cash award.

When it comes to rewarding results, what you say and how you say it really matters. Remember SAIL to ensure a meaningful and clear presentation.

CHAPTER 7

CELEBRATE CAREERS

"Explain your worst manager ever." That was a challenge we extended to our social networks while conducting research for a Forbes article. As you can imagine, we were flooded with responses from people in various industries all over the world.

We heard about bullies. We heard about whiners. We heard about egomaniacs and liars and cheats. However, one of the leaders we heard about didn't sound that bad. In fact, Vinay, who worked for a software company in Delhi, India, explained that his leader and company were excellent, in Vinay's words, at "treating people the right way." In fact, Vinay responded, "I believed I was one of his favorites."

So far, so good. However, then Vinay described how his leader walked a ten-year service award over to his desk while it was still in the shipping package. "He dropped it on my desk. I do not know if he was joking or not but he said, 'Apparently if you keep showing up they send you a gift.' Then he walked away. I was in shock that he would treat me as such. I was hurt and saddened."[1]

Most organizations are good at providing a formal program to recognize their people on the anniversary of their hire date. Unfortunately, we have heard many stories that turn negative when leaders do not adequately acknowledge the employee's contribution to the organization. A prime opportunity exists to highlight the contributions of the employee, and, sadly, it often gets overlooked, underplayed, and marginalized.

Consider your career, your contributions, and your body of work—both inside and outside of your current employer. It means a lot to you. Moreover, it means a lot to those around you—the years of accomplishments, the big projects, and even the accumulated body of work that contributes to your company today.

Now think back to when you started your career. Examine your dreams and your goals. Think about the person you wanted to become—the career you wanted to have and the company you work for. Did you believe you would work at one company for your whole career? The answer is most likely no. Instead you joined a company and hoped it would be the right fit for a few years. You observed your coworkers to see if they were the right team, the values to see if they aligned to yours, and the purpose to understand if this was a company you wanted to continue working for. Either you realized it wasn't the right fit, or through time, realized this was a place where you could make an impact, build strong relationships, and grow to become a leader, because you wanted to feel committed to a cause bigger than yourself.

Now think about your coworkers, employees, and leaders. Do you think they are any different from you? Do you think they want to see their career flourish and become everything they hoped for? Of course they do. Moreover, that is what this chapter focuses on—how much the progression through a career means to an employee, and a leader's opportunity to show their appreciation for it.

We hear it all the time: "People are not interested in building a career with one organization," they say. Alternatively, "Gone are the days of commitment and loyalty between an organization and an individual." Or, "Young people are quick to jump ship and move to the next place that piques their interest."

There's a massive assumption today that employees are not as dedicated. That there's some generational shift that makes people want to change employers often. Or that there's some time frame that employees are willing to stay and that if they do not leave, then their career has become stagnant—they cannot move up the ladder unless they leave.

The reality is entirely different. The truth is people are not just looking to leave—they are seeking to build a career, to do great work, to contribute, and to feel appreciated for those contributions. In fact, our research shows that most employees today aspire to find a place where they feel they fit in, belong, and can build a career.[2]

The U.S. Bureau of Labor Statistics has been tracking employee tenure since 1983. Since 1996, they have surveyed over 60,000 households every two years and published the results. According to their extensive research, the trend indicates employees today are staying longer with their company than they did thirty years ago. In 1983, average employee tenure was around 3.5 years. Fifteen years later, in 1998, people stayed on the job an average of 3.6 years before leaving. In 2014, the average employee stayed 4.6 years with a slight drop in 2016 to 4.2 years, slightly higher than pre-recession levels.[3]

Bureau of Labor Statistics
median tenure with current employer

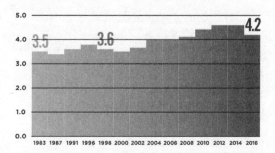

A global quantitative and qualitative study showed that celebrating years of service anniversaries correlated strongly to increased tenure.[4] In fact, organizations that recognize their people for a years of service anniversary keep employees an average of two years longer than organizations that don't. Moreover, if done well, employees stay an average of four years longer than those who do nothing.

Consider the marked difference in study participants' responses when asked how long they planned on staying with their current organization. We were surprised (and it proves how many employees do not have a desire to job-hop) that a new employee estimated they would stay approximately 8.6 years. This is proof that people, when hired, have intentions of staying longer and producing great work. They want to come into an organization and make a difference.

Average number of years an employee plans to stay with their current company.

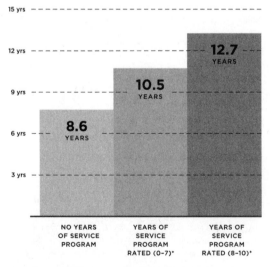

*0 = poor quality program; 10 = high quality program

Notice the marked difference between companies who had a lower-rated service award program and those who had a higher-rated service award program—a more than two-year difference in how long employees estimated they would stay with the company.

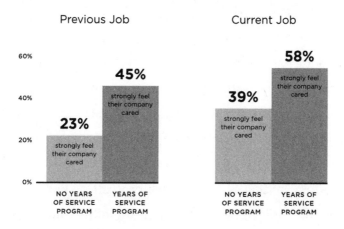

Previous Job   Current Job

*Percentage of employees who strongly feel the company cares about the employees (top 3 box score of 0–10 scale)

In the chart above, notice the increase in employees who firmly believed their company cared about them when they recognized people for their years of service. Respondents were asked to rank both their previous job and their current job on whether or not they believed their company cared about them as an employee.

In both the previous job and the current job there is nearly a 20% increase in employees believing their company cares about them. It is also interesting to consider the marked difference between a previous job and current job—a difference that may signify a foundational human desire to want (and need) to believe that our company cares about us.

Reconsider that story Vinay sent us. Vinay worked for an organization that had a program in place to recognize years of service. He thought he was one of his manager's favorites. However, due to the way his anniversary award was given, Vinay described that manager as his "worst manager ever."

We were not surprised to hear Vinay left his company not long after his poorly handled anniversary. We did not receive any details on his departure, but in an attempt to follow up on his email, we received a response to our attempt to contact him that read, "Our apologies, but Vinay is no longer with the company. Deepak is now handling all of Vinay's clients and would be happy to work with you."

It is a hunch—that is the best we can call it—but our guess is that Vinay did not feel a sense of belonging to the company or team anymore. We are guessing that his manager's pathetic presentation that represented ten years of hard work for the company was Vinay's clue to move on and find a place that appreciated him, where he felt a sense of belonging.

Your job, as a leader, is to ensure you do not have a Vinay leave your team because you are not showing your appreciation and recognizing their important career anniversaries.

WHAT DO WE MEAN BY CELEBRATE A CAREER?

Time, as simple as it may seem, is a complex concept. As much as most of us like to believe that we are the same now as we were five, twenty, or fifty-five years ago, we're not. Experiences, learning, progress, influences, and ideas have changed us through time. A great career is similar. It is built on a timeline of contributions—efforts, experiences, and ideas—as unique as the person who achieved them. These include the little victories. They include the big wins. They include the highest achievements. Moreover, they include all the effort required to create these results. Time and experience change people.

Our research shows that celebrating a career, at any stage:

- Strengthens loyalty.

- Makes people feel respected.

- Shows how they fit in.

- Increases feelings of ownership in the company.

- Creates feelings of connection.

That is a powerful list, which, as a leader, you should be considering at every stage of your team members' careers, even on day one.

What were you thinking on the first day of your job? Most likely you were excited to begin your career. You had high hopes for yourself and the organization you joined. You dreamed of the difference you could make. Moreover, you hoped that people at your new company would welcome you with excitement, open arms, and celebration.

Often when we talk about appreciation, people forget to include the onboarding process. It is the first point in a career where we need to feel appreciated—simply for joining the team. Let's face it; hopefully, all of us were hired because a hiring manager appreciated what we have achieved in the past, the reputation we have built, and the answers we gave during our interview.

Onboarding has recently become a popular topic of conversation. Although we are not going to dive deep into all the specifics of onboarding,[5] we do want to mention it as the beginning of a person's career and critical point to show appreciation. In fact, a study released by the Society for Human Resource Management (SHRM) shows that 90% of employees decide whether or not they will stay with or leave a company in the first six months of their employment.[6] If they elect to stay, the critical nature of celebrating their career only gets more interesting.

We recently conducted a study of people who had been at their jobs from one to thirty years or more to see what we could learn about how time has changed them, the way they perceive the organization, and the way they see their future.[7] Along the way, we discovered some profound insights and universal truths about the psychology of people throughout their careers.

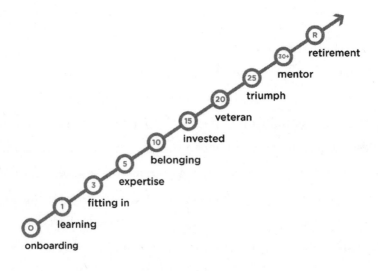

Year 1–The learning phase: In the first year of a person's career, they are like a sponge, soaking up knowledge, details about various personalities, insights into their likes, dislikes, and strengths and weaknesses. After a year on the job, people have made it through the learning curve and started adding value to the team or organization. They are not sure yet what the future holds.

Year 3–Feels like I'm fitting in: By the third year, an employee is getting into the groove of their job, and they are beginning to feel like part of the team. They understand the dynamics of the people they work with. They have made some friends. They have seen how their contributions impact the team, the department, and possibly the organization. Around year three, employees begin to seek growth and become curious about their future opportunities if they decide to stay.

Year 5–I have real expertise: By the fifth year with an organization, people have sacrificed a lot to become an expert and have become more confident. Research shows the five-year mark is a vulnerable time. They often begin wondering, "What's next?" or "Is it time to move on?" They also might be looking for some excitement— the learning portion of their career has slowed, they understand the organization and their role well, and they might be considering a fresh and exciting new start.

Year 10–I belong here: After a decade, employees see their company differently—a psychological shift that changes their perspective. Coworkers, after ten years, are viewed as an extension of their family. Instead of wondering what the organization can do for them, employees at this stage feel truly committed to the cause of the organization and treat the company's goals as their own. They want to win as a team. They defend the company and champion its values.

Year 15–I'm invested: Another psychological shift happens at the fifteen-year mark. By this point, employees have become psychologically invested in building a history with the company and they see lifelong value from the partnership. The company has become part of their identity. They treat the company, and their role, with a personal sense of ownership—watching for waste, seeking to make improvements, and acting as a leader within their sphere of influence. At fifteen years, employees feel grateful toward the organization and want to give back.

Year 20–I lead like a veteran: At twenty years, employees realize they have witnessed a lot of change—both in their personal life and within the company. They have bonded with other long-term employees and their families. They have amassed a wealth of knowledge in their time spent on the job and have gained wisdom and experience that they can impart to younger employees. They collaborate, lead, and inspire the younger workers—not only by showing them what great work looks like in the organization, but also by proving the organization is a great place to do great work.

Year 25–The triumph phase: This, according to research, is an employee's most significant milestone. It is a time when employees celebrate victories both past and present. At twenty-five years, employees still have a lot to contribute. They still are deeply passionate about the organization's future, and they are determined to pass along what they know to the next generation.

Year 30 plus–I am a mentor: Employees who reach the thirty-year mark report an extreme sense of gratitude and indebtedness. They recall their mentors along their journey. They remember the moments where their work was recognized. Moreover, they have a sincere desire to act as a mentor, to go out with a bang, and leave a legacy before they retire, even if it means that just one person in the organization admires them, is grateful for passing along knowledge, or appreciates them specifically for showing them the ropes.

Obviously, we will all vary through each of these phases and need to feel that our career is appreciated in between each of these psychological shifts. Nevertheless, these phases provide a framework for understanding how your employees are feeling in regards to their career with the organization and your team. In fact, our research shows that recognizing and celebrating a person's career achievements impacts the way an employee perceives, feels about, and contributes to an organization.

When celebrating a career, you celebrate:

- The individual by celebrating the whole person and their body of work.

- Their unique value by sharing their successes that bring their personal qualities to life.

- Their talents by pointing out and affirming their inherent capabilities.

- Their roles by denoting their integral role on their team and within the organization.

- Their impact by linking their contributions to building your culture.

You inspire:

- Career commitment by encouraging them to develop a career with your company.

- Conversations by initiating enthusiastic and supportive conversations with their friends and family.

- Peer engagement by inspiring peers to elevate their contributions to the organization and its cause.

You enable:

- Connections by enhancing each leader's awareness of their people and their individual talents.

- Voice by emphasizing the vision and values of the team and company.

From onboarding to retirement, the way employees connect to the organization will change with time and experience. Are they excited and do they feel cared for from the beginning? How are they being treated and recognized for their efforts through the years? Upon retirement, are they looking back with pride or resentment? Moreover, how are their peers viewing the way you celebrate their retirement—are they picturing the day they retire so they can feel just as appreciated? Alternatively, are they wondering if they will be overlooked for all their years of hard work? All of these stages are critical. The bigger question is how to properly celebrate these milestones in someone's career, because with each shift in perception comes a different expectation from the employee—they feel differently about the organization and team, so it should seem obvious that their team and organization should feel differently about them.

HOW SHOULD YOU CELEBRATE CAREERS?

Best practices show that career celebrations are not only critical to keeping and engaging employees, but also inspiring them to perform great work. The top seven suggestions for celebrating careers are:[8]

Make it personal. Who is it for? Nobody wants to stand in a row of nine other people on his or her five-year service anniversary and hear a leader say, "You have all worked here for the same amount of time. Congrats." The recipient of the award should be the only focus. Why would the employee value the experience if the words and presentation are not focused and representative of the contributions they have made? Tell specific stories about the employee's contribution, their projects over time, and their personality. Moreover, tailor your comments to the career stage the recipient is in. A five-year employee will want to hear something different than a fifteen-year employee.

Use tools to remember significant dates. Start by setting clear expectations for yourself and others in your management team to recognize employees on or near their anniversary date. Make it easy by using a system that automatically sends reminders of upcoming years of service anniversaries, tools to plan recognition presentations, invitations to the proper attendees, frameworks to craft the right message, notifications to all parties involved, and guidance to choose the appropriate awards. Using any or all of these tools will help ensure you create a powerful appreciation experience.

The award needs to be appropriate. Our research revealed that employees feel more appreciated and feel a greater sense of loyalty toward their organizations when they received tangible awards—an award that symbolizes the appreciation. An award is a reminder of the work the employee has performed and the appreciation they felt for performing that work. In fact, on a scale of one through seven (with seven equaling "I feel very appreciated by my company") recipients rated the actual award at 4.21, while a presentation of recognition ranked 3.48. Giving an award—along with a personalized presentation that details the work that has been accomplished and the contributions the employee has given to the company or team—boosts the rating up to 6.08. The same research also reported recipients desired awards that satisfied their wants (lifestyle items they might not buy with their own money) versus needs (cash or certificates used to pay bills or some other unmemorable, impersonal purchase).

Sure, most people will say "cash is king" in most situations, but if that money goes home with the employee to pay a plumber or the IRS, it leaves little impression or memory of the work accomplished. If your goal is to celebrate the career milestone and make the recipient feel appreciated, you want to reward them in a way that is memorable and personal. In fact, in our studies, simply by changing a question from, "What would you most want?" to "What would make you feel most appreciated?" we received entirely different answers. When it comes to appreciation, cash is not king. People want something that symbolizes their effort, commitment, contribution, and connection to the company.

In the end, you want to make the entire experience—from select-ing the award to the actual presentation—as personalized as possible.

Make it about them and their contribution, and representative of your appreciation.

The celebration needs to be appropriate. Marriages have anniversaries that matter, and so should careers. Imagine for a second coming home to your spouse and saying, "Here's a rose and a gift certificate to the grocery store for our twenty-fifth wedding anniversary." It is not going to be a good night for you. The same is true at work. Celebrating one or five years of service should feel very different than celebrating twenty-five years. Understanding the emotions and psychology of someone at their one, three, five, ten years (or more) anniversary will help in creating a more personalized and compelling celebration. At ten years or more, consider inviting family members. Valuing these relationships recognizes all those who have sacrificed for, and benefited from, an individual's career contributions. By twenty and twenty-five years, you should make a huge deal of a years of service moment. Employees say that twenty-five years is the most significant milestone and a culmination of all previous milestones. It is a reflective time where employees want to celebrate the career they have had thus far. It is twenty-five years of life. It is a contribution and commitment that deserves praise. You would want to feel appreciated. Make them feel appreciated—appropriately.

Invite others to attend and speak. Consult with the employee being recognized on who should be invited to their celebration. Who should speak? Ask their peers to participate, especially those who know the recipient well and are familiar with his or her contributions. The audience for a career celebration is not just the recipient—it also includes the manager, leaders, peers, and sometimes family or other significant people in their lives.

Realize that most employees will observe numerous years of service presentations before experiencing their own. Most of us have imagined that we are the person being recognized. We have thought about whom we would want at our celebration. We have thought about whom we would want to speak. Through years of service presentations, every member of an audience can embrace the organization's goals and vision, see that their contributions matter as well, and be inspired to do great work. It is a time of reflection and even inspiration for everyone in the room. Leaders can reflect on the contributions of all employees. Leaders reflect on the contributions of the recipient. The recipient reflects on his or her achievements. Audience members and co-workers reflect on their contributions.

Plan your words. If the old saying is true—that people fear public speaking more than they fear death—it is important to plan your words before you give a recognition presentation. Yes, you will have a captive audience. Yes, the room will fall silent because, as we mentioned before, everyone in the room is imagining that they are the person being appreciated, and they are listening closely to your words. Don't worry, however, since most people tell us that when they plan their presentations—they sit down and begin thinking about all the reasons they appreciate the employee being recognized—a flurry of thoughts comes pouring out. Share memorable stories that highlight the recipient's unique qualities and illustrate his or her contributions to the rest of the organization. Talk about what they have accomplished, linking these contributions to your team success and overall values of the organization.

When employees better understand the connection between what they do and achieving company goals, they are more likely to trust their employer. This trust leads to a high level of engagement, enhanced contributions, and commitment. In fact, researchers found employees who were committed to both their immediate work group and the organization had the highest level of collaboration and overall job satisfaction and were least likely to leave. Plan your words. They are more than simple combinations of letters. Words have meaning. They have an impact.

Extend the experience. If you have ever been the recipient of recognition in front of a group, you realize, after all is said and done, that your mind was somewhere else during the presentation. You may have been overwhelmed with emotion. You may have been distracted when you felt all eyes were on you. Moreover, when you try to replay the experience—because it felt so good—in your memory, you simply remember a few fuzzy details that you wish you could relive.

When anyone is recognized, he or she wants the impact of the experience to live on. Moreover, as the person giving the recognition, you want to ensure that your words live on in the employee's mind as well.

Some managers ask a team member to record the event on their smartphone to give the employee a keepsake to save and share with family and friends who could not attend the presentation. During the presentation itself, present a keepsake certificate or symbolic icon with the award to serve as a reminder of the day. Symbolic objects offer reminders of your company's culture, values, and purpose of the organization. They also serve as a reminder to the employee of their efforts, commitment, sacrifices, and specific career achievements. We've seen companies give representative, stylized trophies like oil rigs, trucks,

3D logos, soda cans, and icons representing the individual's work and personal accomplishments. Other companies use keepsakes that match the employee's years of service. Many organizations present printed and online brochures or booklets that include photos of the employee at work, comments of appreciation from coworkers and leaders, and achievements made while they were with the company.

Finally, look for other ways to extend the experience by using social appreciation tools. Internal social tools allow everyone in the organization to celebrate from wherever they might be in the world. Platforms like Twitter, LinkedIn, and Facebook allow the employee's entire community—personal and professional—the chance to offer congratulations. Connecting socially also spotlights your organization as one that values and celebrates its people—inside and outside of the workplace.

VALUE MY WORK AND VALUE ME

Although this book is primarily focused on appreciating people for their great work, it's important to point out that people not only want you to appreciate their efforts, their achievements, and their body of work, but they also want you to appreciate them as a person—the sense of humor, the logical sounding board, the inquisitive mindset, the golf swing, the big fish, the weekend at the waterpark with their children, and, yes, even their cats and dogs.

Career celebrations can spotlight how a person has uniquely impacted the team beyond specific work—through humor, tenacity, thoughtfulness, loyalty or cheer. They can celebrate a person's character—how they have served or watched out for others on the team. They can spotlight how their unique personality and outlook on life has created a better work atmosphere—their positivity, inquisitive nature, grounded mindset, or ability to challenge those around them to better themselves. They can even showcase how their interest in others, their work, their life, their career, and hobbies have created strong relationships and connections that enrich the culture.

With career celebrations, we do not just celebrate the work, we celebrate and show our appreciation for the entire person.

One of the best career recognition examples we have heard was from a guy named Dave, who was celebrating twenty-five years with his company. Dave was known for his work ethic, his desire to get it right, and his tenacity to elevate projects to the next level. Apparently, he had been one of those people who, since the beginning of his career, was not asking the question, "Why?" but instead, "Why not?"

Dave's leader, the CEO, certainly had become close to him throughout his years at work, but Dave did not know how much the CEO knew about his life outside of work. He remembered Dave was a marathon runner. He knew Dave loved and appreciated his husband. Moreover, he was aware that Dave loved spending as much time as he possibly could with his nephews.

To Dave's surprise, the CEO had gone out of his way to invite family and friends that Dave assumed the CEO did not know about. He had researched to find out what Dave's favorite food was and had it catered for the recognition event. The CEO also had a pin created for Dave that represented Dave's history and family legacy at the company (Dave's grandpa had also been an employee). The CEO also collected photos from Dave's family members and had them turned into posters. And, still, this story continues to get better.

"For a CEO to take this type of time to make a difference for me and show me I was important to him gets me through the tough days," Dave said. "Still today."

Dave also mentioned that it was obvious the CEO had thoroughly prepared his presentation. He told detailed stories about hurdles Dave had overcome and that revealed his passion and tenacity to perform great work. He talked about Dave's character, his leadership ability, and his endless energy.

It truly was an impactful presentation—a speech that made everyone attending smile and nod their head in agreement. They all knew exactly what the CEO was talking about as he recognized Dave. But here's the kicker…

After handing Dave his career celebration award, the CEO did something unexpected. "There's one more thing," he said, turning around to grab a few pieces of paper.

The CEO walked over to Dave's two nephews. He squatted to reach eye-level and handed them each a piece of paper. "This is a job application," he said. "If you are anything like your Uncle Dave, I hope you would consider joining this company someday."

Career celebrations embody an employee's efforts, results, and personality traits. They create a relationship at all stages of a career. They retell stories that expose the impact a person has had on the organization and the other people in the organization. They should be celebrated with symbolic awards, personal presentations, and heartfelt words of appreciation.

PREPARE FOR A YEARS OF SERVICE PRESENTATION

When it comes to celebrating careers, presentation is everything! To plan a presentation, think about who the employee being celebrated is, and fill out this worksheet to help you craft a meaningful presentation.

The recipient and milestone (e.g., five years):

Name:_____

Career anniversary:_____

What you appreciate about them as an individual:

_____

_____

_____

_____

_____

_____

_____

_____

_____

_____

Career highlights (Their great work):

_____

_____

_____

_____

_____

_____

_____

_____

_____

The impact on the organization, team, or customer:

_____

_____

_____

_____

_____

_____

_____

_____

_____

The link to organizational values:

_____

_____

_____

_____

_____

_____

_____

_____

The best ways to make it personal:

_____

_____

_____

_____

_____

_____

_____

_____

To download a copy of this form, go to www.octanner.com/appreciatebook.

CELEBRATION CHECKLIST

❑ Schedule the celebration and award presentation as close to the actual anniversary as possible. Celebrations should be for one individual to ensure everything focuses on their great work and contributions to the company.

❑ Invite team members, individuals from other teams they work with, senior leaders, and family members as appropriate. Ask the employee if there are specific people they want to make sure are invited to their presentation.

❑ Select the speakers for the celebration in advance and share tips for what makes a great presentation.

❑ Plan your words. Remember, when you are celebrating a career, you celebrate:

- The individual by celebrating the whole person and their work.

- Their unique value by sharing stories that bring their personal qualities to life.

- Their talents by pointing out and affirming their inherent capabilities.

- Their roles by denoting their integral role on your team and within the entire organization.

- Their impact by linking their contributions to building your team culture.

Ideas to spotlight:

- Talents or hobbies.

- How they have uniquely impacted the team beyond specific work through humor, tenacity, thoughtfulness, loyalty, or cheer.

- Their character or how they have served or watched out for others on the team.

- Their unique personality and outlook on life—their positivity, inquisitive nature, grounded mindset, or ability to challenge those around them for the better.

- Their interest in others, their work, their life, their career, and how they create strong relationships and connections that enrich your team.

❏ Personalize the presentation with a signed card with messages from colleagues. Present a keepsake certificate or symbolic icon and the award selected by the employee.

❏ Think about how to make the celebration personal to the individual and how to extend the experience. You could take pictures, highlight the event in the company newsletter or share it on internal social networks or on Twitter, LinkedIn, or Facebook.

To download a copy of this checklist, go to www.octanner.com/appreciatebook.

QUICK TAKE

Celebrating Careers Achieves Three Distinct Outcomes:

- Encourages the team member to continue to build a career with your team and company
- Inspires employees to become company ambassadors by initiating enthusiastic and supportive conversations with their friends and family
- Engages other employees and inspires them to elevate their contributions.

When You Celebrate, You Are Celebrating:

- Their body of work
- Their unique value to the team, company, and other relationships
- Their talents by affirming their unique skills and attributes
- Their impact and contributions to your team culture

Celebrating A Career Can Be Accomplished By:

- Setting clear expectations that all team members are recognized on or near their anniversary date
- Making the experience personal by sharing positive stories about their work
- Ensuring the celebration is appropriate to the career anniversary they have reached
- Inviting peers to speak
- Planning your words in advance so you can clearly link contributions to your team values and the vision of the company
- Inviting significant others and family members to attend
- Extending the experience by recording the event, taking pictures, and giving the employee a keepsake to save

Frequency:

- Each key career milestone

CHAPTER 8

THE RISE IN VALUE

The sum is always greater than its parts. In this book, you have considered how appreciation has impacted your own life and career—how moments of appreciation have led you to your next challenge and your next piece of great work. You have learned to reset your thinking as a leader, come to understand that your job is to create great results through others, learned how to effectively encourage effort, reward results, and celebrate careers. You have also gained an understanding of how each of these three practices is valuable by itself, but powerful when combined—they build on, support, and elevate one another. Encouraging effort leads to rewarding results, which eventually leads to celebrating successful careers.

We have given you the data, research, and case studies that support the powerful role appreciation can play in influencing others and creating results. Still, what we have not covered is the sum of all these parts—the rise in value.

When a home or piece of fine art rises in value, it is called appreciation. Moreover, when the sum of all the parts of this book are combined into something bigger—for both an organization and an individual—it is called appreciation because there is an undeniable rise in value.

Within this final definition of appreciation, we see a rise in value for your team and entire company, just as so many of the stories have shown a rise in value.

It is one thing to be told about the power of appreciating great work, yet another thing to remember to keep doing it and practicing it. We all talk about building cultures and teams where people are the most valuable assets, but so often we dismiss the opportunities to truly show our appreciation to the very people who want to make a difference and create results. Missing these critical opportunities not only decreases our chances of creating business results, but it also eliminates something a bit more foundational to humanity—the opportunity to show another human being just how much their life is valued.

Jarrett Krosoczka returned as an adult to his former elementary school. That day, he had no idea he would be reintroduced to a woman who would change the trajectory of his career, or that he would play such a significant role in the rest of her life.

Krosoczka is a children's book author and illustrator. Of course, his former elementary school was honored to have a hometown hero back within their walls where his creative imagination was first inspired, honed, and appreciated.

"I noticed, at the back of the room, Jeanie, my lunch lady, and I went to say hello!" he told us during an interview.[1]

Krosoczka and the lunch lady talked about the old days. They talked about Krosoczka's uncle. They talked about many things. And then it was time for Jarrett to talk to the crowd of kids.

"I realized when I was speaking to the group that I had not thought about this lunch lady since elementary school. I thought about all the kids listening to me talk about writing books and illustrating books and how they might not think about the lunch lady either. And that gave me an idea."

Krosoczka told us he thought about the role a lunch lady plays in a child's life—that her job was to feed children every day. He thought about how impressed he was that she remembered him and the fact that she probably remembered a bunch of kids from years past.

"I thought, these are the unsung heroes. . . the people who feed children so we can grow up and do whatever it is we do—run companies, manage people, build products, or write children's books."

A lifelong fan of comic books, Krosoczka decided to create a graphic novel where the heroin was, you guessed it, a lunch lady. The first book in a series of novels, the titular lunch lady uses her fish-stick nunchucks to fight off evil cyborg substitutes, a school bus monster, and mutant mathletes. At the end of every book, the lunch lady captures the bad guy in her hairnet and exclaims, "Justice is served!"

The *Lunch Lady* series is beloved by children around the world, but also by lunch ladies and cafeteria workers, which he did not expect.

"I would visit schools to talk about the books, and the cafeteria staff would participate in a very meaningful way," said Jarrett. "And they would say thank you. From coast to coast, they all said thank you."

Krosoczka loved the appreciation from his readers, but the one who mattered the most to him was Jeanie, his childhood lunch lady.

"I invited Jeanie to my book launch," said Jarrett. "Of course, I gave her a signed copy of the book and a piece of artwork that accompanied the series. She loved it. . . but I did not understand how much she loved it."

Krosoczka's busy life moved forward. He wrote more stories of lunch lady heroism. He told more tales of nunchuck fish sticks. He sold more books. He reaped more praise. Then, two years following the launch of the first *Lunch Lady* book, Krosoczka was informed that Jeanie had passed away.

"I attended the wake," he told us. "Nothing could have prepared me for that day. Next to her casket was the piece of artwork I had given her. Her husband approached and told me that my series meant so much to her because I had acknowledged her hard work and validated what she did for a living."

Again, inspired by Jeanie, Jarrett Krosoczka went home with a new idea—a plan to change cafeterias and the appreciation deserved by cafeteria staff. He created School Lunch Hero Day, a day in which kids appreciate cafeteria employees through creative gestures. Maybe they make hamburger thank-you cards, construction-paper pizza on which each topping is a piece of paper showing gratitude, or drawings of lunch ladies saving the day.

Appreciation is being shared with a group of people, and a profession that never really received appreciation before, all because Jarrett Krosoczka thought to shine a spotlight on a woman he once overlooked.

This last story we want to share is one of the most moving we have heard. It touched us so deeply we knew right when we heard it that we wanted to close this book with it. We hope it stays with you as it did with us.

Martha Elena Moreno Romero was a lifelong resident of Puerto Peñasco, Mexico, a small fishing village that sits at the northern edge of the Sea of Cortez. This single mother of one son was known as a hard worker. She had held numerous jobs throughout her life trying to make ends meet, put food on the table, and feed her growing son. However, the town did not have much to offer in the way of employment.

In 2004, Martha found employment with a U.S. company called Sea Side Reservations, a vacation rental and real estate company headquartered in Arizona. The company, now operating throughout Mexico, was founded by a man named Steve Schwab, who happens to be a friend of Todd's.

"What are you working on now?" asked Steve, as he met Todd for coffee one morning. "Are you working on a book?"

"Yeah, we are doing research on the impact of appreciation in the workplace—how it influences people to create results."

"Do you mean appreciation like showing gratitude toward someone?" asked Steve.

"That is a big part of it. It is about a person feeling appreciated for their contributions—the type of appreciation that somehow touches the human spirit."

Steve paused. "I need to get better at that. I am not bad at it, but because of the language barrier sometimes, I think I could get better."

"We all could get better," replied Todd. "If you have any examples, though—good or bad—I would love to hear them."

Again, Steve paused—longer this time. His eyes wandered off into the distance. It was obvious that he was thinking. It was also obvious that he was thinking of something specific—a story that changed his demeanor.

"Martha," he said, with a nod. "I have the story of Martha. She was a great employee—the best."

"What about her?"

"It is an uncomfortable story," replied Steve. "Martha started with us in the early days as part of our cleaning crew, back when I was just getting started. She was a hard worker. She was great and always willing to do whatever needed to be done, even though she had some health problems." Steve continued, "Over the years I would hear stories about her—about how hard she worked. I would also hear stories about her health. . . and the healthcare system in town, at the time, wasn't very accessible. I took care of some of her medical bills, but, over time, her health caught up with her. She passed away due to difficulties from diabetes."

"That is sad," said Todd.

"It was," replied Steve, still gazing off into the distance. "I did not know her family at all. I knew she had a son. It was one of those times where it felt like a person just disappeared. I could not do anything. But that is when I heard something that shocked me."

"What's that?" asked Todd.

"Martha requested that she be buried in her Sea Side uniform," Steve replied, obviously shaken by his words. "Apparently, as I was told, she never felt so appreciated—by a company and what she called 'her Sea Side family.' That opened my eyes. I never realized we had such an impact. I do not remember everything I ever said to Martha, but I do remember thanking her often and her massive smile when I would. She was awesome. She deserved thanks. She deserved more than thanks. It was obvious that she felt appreciated. I just wish I would have told her more often."

Appreciation is a powerful way to influence greatness. Learn it. Understand it. Practice it. And watch the value increase in the world around you. We see it daily. And, in the end, it can only be described with one single word: beautiful.

ACKNOWLEDGMENTS

This book, although authored by four of us, is the result of many thousands of voices—too many to name them all.

To begin, we must thank the many thousands of survey participants that provided us with the research exposed in this book. Without all these participants giving us their time and honest feedback, we couldn't so boldly proclaim the massive impact appreciation has on mankind's ability to influence greatness.

That being said, we also must thank O.C. Tanner, the O.C. Tanner Institute, and its partners for the combined career opportunities the four of us have been given—for each of us in different ways, a journey around the globe to personally interview both company leaders and employees. It is that opportunity and those conversations which have led us to so many of our questions and directed so many of our research initiatives. For that, we are truly appreciative.

We would also like thank Emily Loose, our content editor, who has a seemingly magical ability to show us where our four minds became jumbled and convoluted during the writing of this book. And a special thanks to Rachel Lyon, our proofreader and indexer, who so brilliantly sees things we all missed.

To our O.C. Tanner Institute research team consisting of Christina Chau, Jordan Rogers, Alex Lovell, and Chris Berry, we owe our extreme gratitude for facilitating, conducting, and analyzing the survey results.

Our creative and design team, including Julia LaPine, Kim Coxey, Chris Drysdale, Chuck Williams, and Scott Arrowood deserve thanks, as they were part of making our findings and final manuscript look fantastic.

Along the way, we have each bounced ideas around with our trusted colleagues and friends, some of whom ended up as stories in this book. These people added great insight, stories, and input that often became turning points of our thinking. Thanks to Scott Archibald, Ed Bagley, Joel Bishop, Jeff Birk, Shauna Bona, Wendy Briggs, Sandra Christensen, Mark Cook, Mindi Cox, Erika Crocker, David Hilton, Scott Jensen, Niel Nickolaisen, Ty Nilsson, Tiffany Noble, Gary Peterson, Kevin Salmon, Scott Sperry, Jarond Suman, Beth Thornton, Elena Todorova, and the late Aimee Wilson, whose contagious spirit left this earth too soon.

To all the friends near and far who responded to our constant questioning through our own social media outlets as we asked about their work, thank you. To the countless professionals around globe who have taken the time to lend us their stories in this book via email, comments online, or via personal conversations at events, thank you for speaking up.

To Dave Petersen, CEO of O.C. Tanner, who passionately believes we can change the world and influence greatness in all of our work through appreciation, we say "thank you."

This book is a product of many voices. But it would not exist without our biggest champion, our publisher, Alisha Newbold. She was our shepherd as the four of us would often drift away from the focal point during countless meetings, or drift away from our schedule. Alisha, you consistently place us all in a state of awe by your talent, your organizational skill, your insights, and your tenacity.

We'd also like to thank our families who have supported us through this lengthy process. They have all spent far too much time listening to the stories we tell, hearing the latest survey results, and answering our questions about appreciation in their own lives and careers. We hope that all of our research helps us become better at sharing our appreciation with you, our spouses and children, as you all are the most important people in our lives.

Finally, we'd like to thank all of you who have, knowingly or unknowingly, influenced greatness in someone else by showing your appreciation for them or their work. It is you, and your words, that have made the world a more beautiful and extraordinary place to accomplish something great.

IS IT BETTER TO GIVE THAN TO RECEIVE?

We're all familiar with the time-tested adage "It's better to give than to receive." Now we have science to back that up that statement.

This O.C. Tanner Institute study examines not only the powerful benefits of employee recognition, but more specifically, how giving recognition effects the giver. It turns out, giving recognition is directly linked to some pretty profound results—an increase in engagement, innovation and work results. Take a glimpse at what we found.

Employees who give recognition experience:

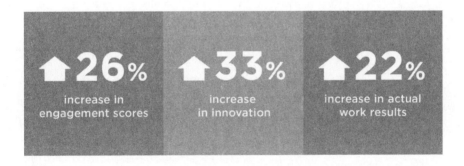

Find the full paper here: http://www.octanner.com/better-to-give

INFLUENCING GREATNESS: GIVING, RECEIVING, AND OBSERVING RECOGNITION

Organizations have a unique opportunity to influence the greatness that is inherently found in everyone. One of the most effective levers senior leaders can use to attract, retain, and engage employees is recognition. While the benefits of recognition are often solely attributed to the person receiving recognition, this study demonstrates that a combination of giving recognition, receiving recognition, and observing recognition is more impactful on individual employees than any single part of the recognition experience.

The gains of recognition culture are clear, and organizations should reevaluate how they can better nurture a culture that fosters recognition, not just for the recipients' sake, but also for those giving it and those observing it. When you compare employees who never participate in the full recognition experience with those who always participate, we find the following increases in engagement, wellbeing, innovation, and results:

591% the percentage of employees who are engaged

420% the percentage of employees who have "excellent" wellbeing

536% increase in the percentage of employees innovating

571% the percentage of employees who have "excellent" work results

This impact is also incremental in nature. There is almost a three-times increase across all the metrics when comparing the worst at giving, receiving, and observing recognition to employees who are in between.

Find the full paper here: http://www.octanner.com/give-receive-observe

THE EFFECT OF PERFORMANCE RECOGNITION ON EMPLOYEE ENGAGEMENT

Think about the last time someone you work with told you "Great job!" How did it make you feel? And what did it make you want to do? For most of us, sincere recognition of strong performance can be a powerful motivator to redouble our efforts and strive for even greater performance in the future, whether in sports, among our families, or at work. In fact, global research commissioned by the O.C. Tanner Institute and conducted by the Cicero Group shows that employees receiving strong performance recognition are much more likely to be highly engaged at their job and, as a result, are more likely to perform at their maximum output and develop innovative ways to improve their company. In fact, look at the differences in engagement between employees who receive strong performance recognition compared with weak performance recognition.

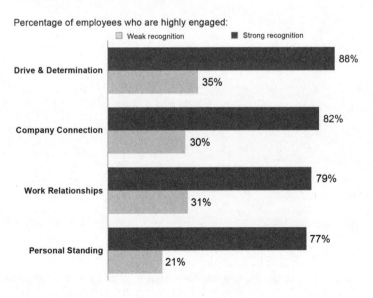

Percentage of employees who are highly engaged:

☐ Weak recognition   ■ Strong recognition

Drive & Determination
88%
35%

Company Connection
82%
30%

Work Relationships
79%
31%

Personal Standing
77%
21%

In this white paper you'll also discover:

- Why well-recognized employees have more drive and determination.

- How performance recognition impacts innovation.

- Why informal, day-to-day recognition for effort increases employee confidence.

- How formal, above-and-beyond recognition can increase customer service levels.

THE BUSINESS CASE FOR RECOGNITION

Looking to get executive buy-in and support of a proposed recognition program? Highlighting research from the O.C. Tanner Institute, along with the latest Gallup and Aon Hewitt studies, this white paper demonstrates how effective recognition has been proven to:

- Result in great work

- Increase engagement

- Encourage innovation and productivity

- Improve trust and manager relationships

- Attract and retain talent

The most significant statistic from this research was that 37% of respondents identified recognition as the most important thing their leader or company could do to cause them to produce great work. That percentage was nearly three times larger than that of any other response in the survey.

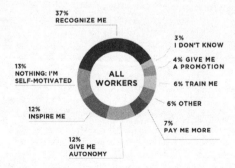

Find the full paper here: http://www.octanner.com/recognition-businesscase

THE IMPACT OF EXCELLENT EMPLOYEE WELLBEING

Leaders and human resource professionals around the globe have an ever-increasing focus on employee wellbeing. Companies in every industry have crafted initiatives to improve employee wellness and boost productivity and employee satisfaction as a result. But why do these initiatives often struggle to make a lasting impact on employee lifestyles? How can organizations better understand and affect holistic employee wellbeing?

Global O.C. Tanner Institute research, surveying over 2,000 employees, explored answers to these questions including:

- The difference between wellness and wellbeing—and why leaders who don't understand the distinction are missing a bigger picture.

- How to build initiatives that drive improvement in holistic employee wellbeing by encouraging healthy behaviors in three key areas of wellness.

- The significant benefits in store for companies that effectively improve employee wellbeing.

- Why as employee wellbeing increases, its positive effects resonate throughout the organization and teams become more productive, more collaborative, and better prepared to innovate.

- How wellbeing affects individuals, teams, and results throughout an organization—even measurably impacting its bottom line.

However, most interesting was the following. Notice how, amongst the scope of traditional benefits, recognition plays a crucial role.

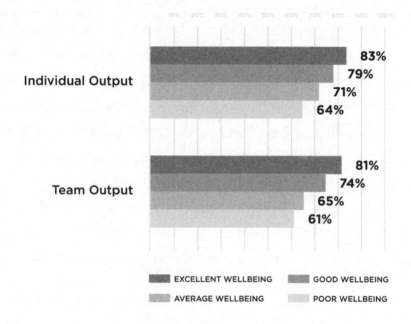

ENABLING GREAT WORK

Good work keeps a business going. Great work takes companies to the next level. This white paper examines not only what great work is, but how to promote great work in your team. After all, great work doesn't just help your company thrive, it helps give each employee a sense of purpose, achievement, and appreciation for their own work.

Highlights from this white paper:

- Chasing engagement doesn't necessarily inspire great work. Human nature works the other way around—great work inspires engagement.

- Managers tend to believe great work is for those at the top of their organizations while non-managers believe innovating is for everyone. Translation: smart leaders share great work opportunities with their team.

- The resource gap—make sure people have the basic resources they need to transform good work into great work.

How can the 5 Great Work Skills help produce great work in your organization?

Find the full paper here: http://www.octanner.com/great-work-index

NOTES AND RESOURCES

CHAPTER 1: IT'S UNIVERSAL

[1] http://www.dictionary.com/browse/appreciate

[2] "The Unique Story of Beethoven's Ninth Symphony," David Nelson, August 2, 2012. http://inmozartsfootsteps.com/2472/the-unique-story-of-beethovens-ninth-symphony/

[3] Coldplay's Twitter Account, April 22, 2016. https://twitter.com/coldplay/status/723652553913724928

[4] "Holy now! 108 years later, Cubs best in World," Carrie Muskat, November 3, 2016. http://m.mlb.com/news/article/207995060/cubs-win-world-series-after-108-years-waiting/

[5] "Bulgaria Presents in Paris Prehistoric Drawings From Magura Cave with Photo Exhibit," Ivan Dikov, July 3, 2016. http://archaeologyinbulgaria.com/2016/07/03/bulgaria-presents-in-paris-prehistoric-drawings-from-magura-cave-with-photo-exhibit/

[6] "Sydney Opera House,"www.australia.gov.au/about-australia/australian-story/sydney-opera-house

[7] National Park Service, "Edouard de Laboulaye," https://www.nps.gov/stli/learn/historyculture/edouard-de-laboulaye.htm

[8] Tribute to great men-Noble square, Cape town, http://www.southafrica.net/za/en/articles/entry/article-southafrica.net-nobel-square-cape-town

[9] "7 Things You May Not Know About Ticker-Tape Parades," By Jacqueline Purdy, July 10, 2015. http://www.history.com/news/history-lists/7-things-you-may-not-know-about-ticker-tape-parades

[10] "MOF Chocolatier 2015: Not awarded!" Jaume Cot, February 18, 2015. www.sogoodmagazine.com/pastry-blog/pastry-competition/mof-chocolatier-2015-not-awarded/

[11] Honouring achievement and celebrating success. https://www.royal.uk/honouring-achievement-and-celebrating-success

[12] "What Does a Grateful Brain Look Like," Adam Hoffman, November 16, 2015. http://greatergood.berkeley.edu/article/item/what_does_a_grateful_brain_look_like

[13] "Influencing Greatness: Giving, Receiving, and Observing Recognition," www.octanner.com/landing/offers/giving--receiving--and-observing-recognition.html

CHAPTER 2: THE ONE THING

[1] "What Causes People To Produce Great Work," http://www.octanner.com/landing/offers/drivers-of-great-work.html

[2] "Healthcare: Using Recognition to Confront a Crisis," http://www.octanner.com/institute/white-papers/healthcare-using-recognition-to-confront-a-crisis.html

[3] "The Effect of Performance Recognition on Employee Engagement," http://www.octanner.com/landing/impact-of-performance-recognition.html

[4] "Healthcare: Using Recognition to Confront a Crisis," www.octanner.com/institute/white-papers/healthcare-using-recognition-to-confront-a-crisis.html

[5] Dow Chemical, www.octanner.com/clients/dow-chemical.html

[6] "Jim Carrey," https://en.wikipedia.org/wiki/Jim_Carrey

[7] "Jim Carrey's commencement address at the 2014 MUM Graduation," https://www.youtube.com/watch?v=V80-gPkpH6M

8 "The Great Work Index," www.octanner.com/landing/
offers/2016-great-work-index.html

CHAPTER 3: THE WORK OF A LEADER

1 The NBA at 50, http://www.nba.com/history/
players/50greatest.html

2 "Great Players That Were Bad Coaches In Sports,"
www.nbcsports.com/great-players-were-bad-coaches-
sports#slide-4

3 "Why Great Managers Are So Rare," Randall Beck and
Jim Harter, March 25, 2014. http://www.gallup.com/
businessjournal/167975/why-great-managers-rare.aspx

4 "Ferguson's Formula," Anita Elberse, October 2013 Issue.
https://hbr.org/2013/10/fergusons-formula

5 "Six Qualities Leaders Need to Be Successful,"
Melanie Greenberg, Ph.D, April 06, 2012. https://www.
psychologytoday.com/blog/the-mindful-self-express/201204/
six-qualities-leaders-need-be-successful

6 "The Trickle-Down Effect of Good (and Bad) Leadership,"
Jack Zenger and Joseph Folkman, January 14, 2016. https://
hbr.org/2016/01/the-trickle-down-effect-of-good-and-bad-
leadership

7 "The Trickle-Down Effect of Good (and Bad) Leadership,"
Jack Zenger and Joseph Folkman, January 14, 2016. https://
hbr.org/2016/01/the-trickle-down-effect-of-good-and-bad-
leadership

8 "How To Lead Extreme Growth," David Sturt and Todd
Nordstrom, July 29, 2014. http://www.forbes.com/sites/
davidsturt/2014/07/29/3-promises-to-drive-extreme-growth-
ceo-coach-sheldon-harris-spills-the-beans/

9 "Emotional Connection Is The Heart Of Leadership, Right?"
David Sturt and Todd Nordstrom, August 5, 2015. http://
www.forbes.com/sites/davidsturt/2015/08/05/emotional-
connection-is-the-heart-of-leadership-right/

[10] "Global research: The Great Work Study," http://www.
octanner.com/content/dam/oc-tanner/documents/global-
research/Great-Work-Study.pdf

[11] Abrashoff, D. Michael. 2012. *It's Your Ship: Management
Techniques from the Best Damn Ship in the Navy*. New York:
Grand Central Publishing.

[12] "Death Valley Exposed: Wildflowers - February 2016,"
https://www.youtube.com/watch?v=LJbcWFTBn08

[13] "The Great Work Index," http://www.octanner.com/landing/
offers/2016-great-work-index.html

CHAPTER 4: HOW AND WHAT DO YOU APPRECIATE

[1] "The Positive Perspective: Dr. Gottman's Magic Ratio" By Ellie
Lisitsa, December 5, 2012.

[2] Bailey, Sebastian, and Octavius Black. 2016. *Mind Gym:
Achieve More By Thinking Differently*. San Francisco:
HarperOne.

[3] Lotus of Siam, 953 E. Sahara Ave, Suite A5, Las Vegas, NV
89104, www.lotusofsiamlv.com

CHAPTER 5: ENCOURAGE EFFORT

[1] "Influencing Greatness: Giving, Receiving, and Observing
Recognition. http://www.octanner.com/landing/offers/giving--
receiving--and-observing-recognition.html

[2] "The ROI Of Effective Recognition," http://www.octanner.
com/content/dam/oc-tanner/documents/white-papers/O.C.-
Tanner_Effective-Recognition-White-Paper.pdf

[3] Sturt, David. 2013. *Great Work*: How to Make a Difference
People Love. New York: McGraw Hill Education.

[4] As business partners with Virgin Trains, their HR team shared
content with O.C. Tanner.

5 "The ROI Of Effective Recognition," http://www.octanner.com/content/dam/oc-tanner/documents/white-papers/O.C.-Tanner_Effective-Recognition-White-Paper.pdf

6 "How Failing Can Lead to Future Success" podcast, http://blog.octanner.com/insights/gwi047-jay-samit

CHAPTER 6: REWARD RESULTS

1 "The Impact of Performance Recognition," http://www.octanner.com/landing/impact-of-performance-recognition.html

CHAPTER 7: CELEBRATE CAREERS

1 Collected as part of research for a *Forbes* article. https://www.forbes.com/sites/davidsturt/2014/08/14/the-worst-bosses-might-actually-be-good-for-your-career/

2 "Celebrate Careers," http://www.octanner.com/landing/celebrate-careers.html

3 http://www.bls.gov/news.release/pdf/tenure.pdf

4 "The Effect of Years of Service Award Programs: Quantifying the Return-On-Investment," http://www.octanner.com/landing/awards-programs.html

5 "Onboarding: Early Engagement Through Recognition," http://www.octanner.com/institute/white-papers/onboarding-early-engagement-through-recognition.html

6 "Onboarding Key to Retaining, Engaging Talent," Roy Maurer, April 16, 2015. https://www.shrm.org/resourcesandtools/hr-topics/talent-acquisition/pages/onboarding-key-retaining-engaging-talent.aspx

7 "Celebrating Careers," http://www.octanner.com/landing/celebrate-careers.html

8 "Celebrating Careers," http://www.octanner.com/landing/celebrate-careers.html

CHAPTER 8: THE RISE IN VALUE

[1] "Episode #53 Jarret Krosoczka Great Work Insights,"
https://www.youtube.com/watch?v=sxuq55GdENs

ABOUT THE AUTHORS

With a combined century of hands-on experience leading, researching, analyzing, interviewing, and publishing, each author of *Appreciate* has been applauded as a thought leader in their respective specialities.

David Sturt

Author of the *New York Times* Best Seller *Great Work*, David's articles and interviews are frequently published in *Forbes, Harvard Business Review, Fortune, Entrepreneur* and NPR. He has spoken at TEDx and to thousands of leaders at conferences and companies all over the world. David has two decades of experience in research, innovation, and leadership. He was born in England, raised in South Africa, and educated in the U.S. and Asia.

Todd Nordstrom

As host of the popular "Great Work Insights" podcast, weekly contributor to Forbes.com, Inc.com, and Director for the O.C. Tanner Institute, Todd's career is full of insight based on thousands of in-depth interviews from around the globe. He has spoken to a wide range of audiences, from introducing rock bands in arenas to on-air interviews with c-suite leaders and conference breakout sessions.

Kevin Ames

With a mission to instill in others a passion for personal and professional excellence, Kevin Ames is an author, a world-renowned speaker, and a Director for the O.C. Tanner Institute. He has spoken to hundreds of companies, leadership groups, executive teams, and conferences world wide. Kevin is an expert in the areas of workplace culture, engagement, teambuilding, leadership, and personal development. His presentations have been called, "clear, dynamic, insightful, honest, and informative."

Gary Beckstrand

Gary brings twenty-eight years of research, marketing, and business development experience to O.C. Tanner. He has consulted with many Fortune 100 companies to assess recognition cultures, develop strategic solutions, and measure results. Prior to joining O.C. Tanner, Gary managed many well-known brands for global organizations, including Frito-Lay, Kellogg's, and Franklin Covey.

ABOUT THE O.C. TANNER INSTITUTE

O.C. Tanner Institute

The O.C. Tanner Institute conducts research and publishes insights that help organizations attract, engage, and retain top talent by becoming great places to work. The Institute provides a global forum for exchanging ideas about recognition, engagement, leadership, culture, human values, corporate wellbeing, and sound business principles that influence greatness.

octanner.com/institute.html

O.C. Tanner

For nearly a century, the O.C. Tanner Company has been helping companies around the globe appreciate employees who do great work—by encouraging effort, rewarding results, and celebrating careers. Through innovative technology, proven expertise, and impeccable client care, O.C. Tanner helps many of the world's largest and most recognized people engage and celebrate their people.

octanner.com

INDEX

If you enjoyed *Appreciate: Celebrating People, Inspiring Greatness,* check out our breakthrough *New York Times* best-seller *Great Work: How to make a difference people love.*

This book proves that anyone, from any background, can make a difference people love. Discover the five skills to make it happen.

Available at online retailers and in bookstores.
greatwork.com

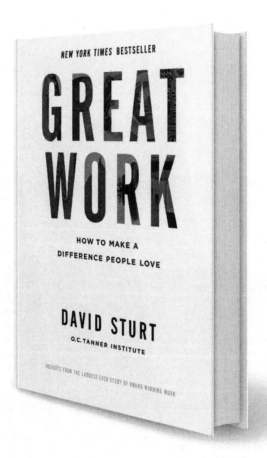